"What makes a leader? Is it a com it style? Is it a certain way of communicating? What do leaders do that makes people perceive them as leaders?

If you are a leader of a company or aspire to be one – this book is a 'must have'. Ronald Tay has written an important book with inspiring leadership stories that provides a unique overview of what it takes to be a leader. This is easy to read, insightful and informative for any leader, drawing on unprecedented personal access and a keen sense of the dynamics of leaders' institutions and their personal lives. It also shows how to create the conditions for inspiring future generations of leaders to seek passion and purpose."

PROF SATTAR BAWANY
CEO & C-Suite Master Executive Coach
Centre for Executive Education (CEE)

"What I like most about *Leadership Conversations* is that these are dialogues with experienced leaders rather than academics, which Ronald Tay has skilfully consolidated into a valuable learning tool.

Their comments and advice stem from being in the real leadership 'hot seat' and not from abstract theories. While the perspectives are varied, some key common leadership themes emerge. I especially like the way in which 'ideas' have been captured at intervals, to reinforce the messages. A novel approach to leadership learning, based on genuine in-depth experiences."

IAIN MARTIN
Chairman, I.J. Martin & Co Ltd
Author of *Looking Down on Leaders: a bird's eye view of business and bosses*

"Three things make this book unique. First, it offers a perspective that truly reflects leadership in Asia, and all of the business and cultural nuances that this entails. Second, within the context of Asia, it has excellent diversity in terms of the people and organisatons featured to provide a broad perspective. Finally, it doesn't just focus on what successful people currently do but how they got to where they are. Overall, a very compelling and practical guide to becoming a successful leader in Asia."

PATRICK FEI
Managing Director, BTS Asia Pacific

"There is no one recipe for inspirational leadership, Ronald's second book is a fantastic insight into how real leaders make it happen and the journey and lessons they go through. This is a must read if you like to learn through stories and you are positioning yourself as a future leader or you need some extra incentive to get your leadership role back on track."

MOIRA ROBERTS
Head of Human Resources, UBS Singapore

"This book is an excellent collection of impactful and practical ideas for leading oneself, others and an organisaton. The insights shared here are deeply relevant for leaders across levels and professional fields. I would recommend it to any existing or aspiring leader."

RAJIV VIJ
Leadership Coach & author of *Discovering Your Sweet Spot*

"This book is quite simply a game-changing 'Tour de Force' in our understanding of Universal Leadership – a remarkable achievement and essential reading for anyone with an interest in or a role as a leader.

Ronald Tay's excellent insights through his conversations with real leaders show how universal is the principle that leaders are defined by their actions, not by their geography, culture, upbringing or education. Gone are the clichés and laboured attempts to label leadership styles as geographically dependent. As Matthew Lang says in the book, and I agree: 'the fundamentals of leading a team here are no different to leading a team in Africa, Europe, America or anywhere else in the world.'

Ronald's sensitive questioning and listening style reveal how important the leader's actions are in helping people become superheroes by creating role clarity and showing value for everyone."

JIM HICK
Singapore Country Manager, Impact International

"In *Leadership Conversations*, Ronald Tay has compiled an outstanding collection of interviews with 16 smart, interesting, and experienced leaders. Every page is filled with the kind of rare wisdom that can only come from years of leading at the front lines of organisations. A must-read for anyone aspiring to, or already in, a position of leadership!"

BRENDA BENCE
Senior Executive Coach and award-winning author of eight books, including *Would YOU Want to Work for YOU?*

LEADERSHIP
CONVERSATIONS

16 leading professionals
share the secrets of
their success

RONALD TAY

Marshall Cavendish
Editions

© 2015 Marshall Cavendish International (Asia) Pte Ltd

Published in 2015 by Marshall Cavendish Editions
An imprint of Marshall Cavendish International
1 New Industrial Road, Singapore 536196

The publisher makes no representation or warranties with respect to the contents of this book, and specifically disclaims any implied warranties or merchantability or fitness for any particular purpose, and shall in no events be liable for any loss of profit or any other commercial damage, including but not limited to special, incidental, consequential, or other damages.

Other Marshall Cavendish Offices: Marshall Cavendish Corporation. 99 White Plains Road, Tarrytown NY 10591-9001, USA • Marshall Cavendish International (Thailand) Co Ltd. 253 Asoke, 12th Flr, Sukhumvit 21 Road, Klongtoey Nua, Wattana, Bangkok 10110, Thailand • Marshall Cavendish (Malaysia) Sdn Bhd, Times Subang, Lot 46, Subang Hi-Tech Industrial Park, Batu Tiga, 40000 Shah Alam, Selangor Darul Ehsan, Malaysia.

Marshall Cavendish is a trademark of Times Publishing Limited

National Library Board, Singapore Cataloguing-in-Publication Data
Tay, Ronald, author.
Leadership conversations : 16 leading professionals share the secrets of their success / Ronald Tay. – Singapore : Marshall Cavendish Editions, 2015.
pages cm
ISBN : 978-981-4561-50-1 (paperback)
1. Leadership. 2. Success. I. Title.

HD57.7
658.4092 – dc23   OCN907204767

Printed in Singapore by Markono Print Media Pte Ltd.

CONTENTS

9 —— FOREWORD

12 —— INTRODUCTION

"Leading with patience and drive"
15 **JONATHAN ASHERSON**
Regional Director, ASEAN and Pacific, Rolls-Royce

"Being the game-changer"
29 **ALAN CHAN**
Chief Executive Officer, Singapore Press Holdings (SPH)

"Be authentic and stand for something"
45 **PHYLLIS CHEUNG**
Managing Director, McDonald's China

"Leaders do well by doing good"
62 **KOH POH TIONG**
Chairman and Senior Advisor of Ezra Holdings
Board Member of Fraser and Neave Limited

"Clarity in purpose and communication"
72 **KWEK KOK KWONG**
Chief Executive Officer, NTUC Learning Hub

"Bringing out the best in your team"

85 **MATTHEW LANG**
Corporate Vice President and Head of Southeast Asia & Oceania CU, Sony Mobile Communications

"Little gestures create big impact"

103 **CAROL FONG**
Chief Executive Officer, CIMB Securities

"Daring to disrupt"

115 **ROD LEAVER**
Chief Executive Officer, Asia, Lend Lease

"Responsibility to the people"

128 **SYLVIA LIM**
Chairman, Workers' Party

"Leading the profession"

143 **MAX LOH**
Managing Partner for ASEAN and Singapore, EY

"Leading collaboratively"

164 **ARNOUD DE MEYER**
President, Singapore Management University

"Servant leadership"

175 **JACK SIM**
Founder, World Toilet Organisation

"Inculcate a strategic vision to drive change"

192 **BERNARD TAN KOK KIANG**
President, Commercial Business Group,
Singapore Technologies Kinetics Ltd

"Build trust as a leader'"

210 **TAN CHUAN JIN**
Minister of Manpower and Minister for Social and Family
Development, Singapore

"Lead with humility, then wisdom"

220 **DR WILLIAM WAN**
General Secretary, Singapore Kindness Movement

"Embrace diversity"

240 **ALICIA YI**
Managing Director, Korn Ferry

261   **CONCLUSION:**
LEADERSHIP IN PERSPECTIVE

286   **ACKNOWLEDGEMENTS**

287   **ABOUT THE AUTHOR**

FOREWORD

Few would argue that the environment we operate in today is increasingly volatile, uncertain, complex and ambiguous (or VUCA, a term first coined by the US Army War College to describe the unpredictable security environment of the late 1990s). Coupled with the technology revolution that has changed our way of life and impacted how organisations are run, the leader today faces a whole new set of challenges. The leader is constantly faced with a deluge of data, connected with both internal and external stakeholders 24/7, faces unrelenting public scrutiny, and yet is required to exhibit the right behaviours and make the right decisions each time, all the time. Leading an organisation today, regardless of whether it is a private corporation, the public sector, a non-profit organisation, or an academic institution, has become so much more challenging.

That said, from the interviews in the book, it is heartening to see that there are powerful leadership principles and behaviours that are timeless, that leaders cannot succeed without their teams, that leaders still need to spend time to engage and motivate their people, perhaps even more so in this digital era. It is also interesting to note that many of these leaders were shaped by crucible experiences in their youth, and very often, had to deal with adversity at a very young age. In the early stages of their career, many were given opportunities to take on stretched roles/overseas assignments, which gave them a head start in their careers and subsequently helped shape their leadership philosophy. Another common trend is that these leaders have lived and worked across various countries and cultures, which greatly contributed to their ability to balance progressive Western leadership practices with the traditional wisdom of Asian leadership principles.

In the same vein, our research at the Human Capital Leadership Institute highlights a number of common strategies that successful leaders employed to get to where they are. First, successful leaders make long-term career plans but remain open to possibilities. They appreciate that the path to the top is not necessarily straightforward and what drove them was an impetus to grow in their profession by constantly stretching their talents and expanding their frames of reference. Secondly, we found that successful leaders actively looked for international assignments early in their careers. The third developmental strategy that was common to successful leaders was their exposure to cross-functional experiences and taking on risky/tough assignments in the early stages of their career. At the same time, these leaders proactively build a wide and deep support network. These networks are both within and external to their organisaton, and these are people whom they can turn to for advice, who provide input as coaches and mentors. The last aspect we found common to many successful leaders was their humility and openness, to readily admit when they were wrong, to be upfront when they do not have the answer, to be authentic, and to constantly seek feedback from their team.

In *Leadership Conversations*, Ronald has put together 16 very personal and powerful stories of leaders representing a cross section of the corporate world, academia, non-profit organisations and even from the political arena to showcase the endearing values that anchor these leaders' actions, and a multitude of effective leadership practices. These stories and experiences truly resonate with the work that HCLI does, and the more we have these stories documented and shared with the wider community, the more we learn about effective leadership in our part of the world.

I believe each and every reader would find something in this book that truly resonates, and more importantly, be motivated to want to be a better leader of a team, an organisaton or a community.

Kwan Chee Wei
Chief Executive Officer
Human Capital Leadership Institute
May 2015

INTRODUCTION

As you pick up this book, you are probably thinking to yourself, "why would we need another book talking about leadership?" Indeed, a quick search on Google for the word "leadership" generates over 476 million hits within 0.38 seconds. Anyone that is interested in the topic of leadership would not have to take too much effort to find leadership conferences taking place in their city, watch videos of leadership gurus expounding their theories, or even certify themselves as a leadership coach!

With such prevalence of leadership resources out there, it may seem surprising why a startling 86% of respondents to the Survey on the Global Agenda agree that we have a leadership crisis in the world today. As there are many more leaders appointed each day, you will also hear of more incidences of failing leaders who are involved in some form of scandal, inept in managing themselves and their organisations, or plain nasty ones who place their own interests ahead of those they are meant to be leading. We passionately love or hate our leaders simply because of one fact: that people want to be led. We want leaders with human values and respect for people's unique talents and the contributions they can make. Employees want leaders who will create an environment that nurtures excellence, risk taking and creativity. We do not need leaders because society tells us we do, and we do not need leaders because our employers enforce it upon us, we need leaders simply because we are born with a natural desire to be led. We are predisposed with a need to be guided, nurtured and supported throughout our lives at all levels and in all situations. And when we are fortunate enough to find a leader that encompass these traits, our lives and behaviors can literally be changed forever.

My first life-changing experience with such a leader was my Primary Four form teacher Mrs Peggy Ang. Back then I was a 10-year old coping with the angst of puberty, struggling to keep up with my grades and had no clue what my strengths and weaknesses were. Mrs Ang had the unique ability of seeing beyond my insecurities, asked me to take over the class as class monitor and encouraged me to excel first in the subjects that I was good at, then to work on the ones I was weaker in. She spent extra hours coaching and encouraging me as well as even inviting me to her family for occasional meals. Gradually I found myself gaining self-esteem, improving my grades to advance to the top class in Primary Five and eventually becoming a "leader" myself as class monitor and school prefect. That is the unique distinguishing trait about great leaders: the ability to look beyond what we are capable of and inspire us to work towards a better version of ourselves.

Through the years, I have been blessed by many other leaders and mentors that have taught me valuable lessons of leadership – many of which I have learnt either through observing them in action, or the experiences they have been generous enough to share with me to shortcut my learning process. In my first book entitled *Career Conversations*, I interviewed 20 professionals on their insights to a successful career in their respective industry fields. In this second publication on *Leadership Conversations*, it is my ardent wish that through the insights of these 16 CEOs that you will find practical advice (that will also shortcut your learning process) towards leading yourself, others and your organisaton to excellence as well as stirring action towards becoming a better version of yourself as a leader today.

Godspeed on your own leadership journey – I know I am still very much working on my own better version everyday!

Ronald Tay

JONATHAN ASHERSON
Regional Director, ASEAN and Pacific
Rolls-Royce

LEADING WITH PATIENCE & DRIVE

JONATHAN ASHERSON is a Chartered Engineer with a BSc (Hons) degree in Mechanical Engineering. Before moving to Singapore in March 1999, he was the Regional Executive for Rolls-Royce in Kuala Lumpur, Malaysia, and was appointed Regional Director on 29 November 2012.

He joined Rolls-Royce from Siemens AG in 1995, where he was Head of the Regional Competence Centre for Industrial Power, Asia Pacific and based in Kuala Lumpur after having worked in Germany, the USA, China and Malaysia for 15 years.

Jonathan currently sits on a range of advisory committees for various educational and research institutions in Singapore, is a board member of the Singapore International Chamber of Commercial (SICC) and a past president of the Singapore British Chamber of Commerce. He was a board member of the

Economic Development Board of Singapore (EDB) from 2007 to 2011, as well as an advisor to the Singapore Institute of International Affairs (SIIA). He sits on the Steering Committee of the Applied Study in Polytechnic and ITE Review (ASPIRE).

Jonathan received an OBE in 2007 and was conferred the Public Service Medal (Friends of Singapore) Award under the Singapore National Day Awards 2010.

He was awarded an honorary Doctorate of Science from Kingston University in 2010.

LEADING YOURSELF

What is your career history and what led to your being appointed as the regional CEO of Rolls-Royce?

I first started working for Siemens in Germany. I've worked for large multinational companies throughout my life – 15 years for Siemens and 20 years for Rolls-Royce. At the Siemens headquarters, I received good grounding for a few years. I was in a technical sales role, and held a completely global portfolio with almost no domestic activity. I was then sent to solve a particular market related issue in America for a year. Although it was a large company, I was pioneering for a small division in the company, and enjoyed that very much. The company then wanted to do something similar in China, and so I put my hand up and they sent me to China in the 1980s. I was there for three years and later identified that I wanted to continue working in Asia, despite not knowing much about the region.

How did your stint in Asia begin?

I first proposed that my division begin looking at Asia as a market from within Asia itself. The proposal was accepted and I was sent to Singapore in the early 1990s. I then established Asia-Pacific sales marketing and related services activity for that division and we later moved marketing for the division to Kuala Lumpur, where I worked to expand our business. I was then recruited by Rolls-Royce to open their first office in Malaysia. I went from an organisation with 7,800 people in Siemens Malaysia to just one manager in Rolls-Royce. After a few years in Malaysia, I moved to Singapore to head the representative office. There were seven people here handling various activities and we had previously secured the Singapore Airlines account. We then looked at what we do from a Singapore-based viewpoint and expanded it to be progressively regional in terms of our industrial strategy, in partnership with joint ventures established in maintenance and repair with the airline and technology. In the process, we've grown over the last 15 years to over 2,500 people and are serving one of our biggest customers in the world.

I've had the same business card since I joined the company in 1995 in Malaysia, but they've added various countries to form a region now. I first started here as a regional director with seven people, but now I am the regional director with a substantial team established in Singapore across sectors with activity ranging from technical services, manufacturing, customer support, technology acquisition and operational and corporate functions.

Did you have any leadership role models who inspired you? What are some of the lessons you've learnt from them?

My starting point is a cliché. My father led an electricity state organisation in Africa then and I was looking for an easy way to get a holiday job. I thought that surely my father could get me one in his organisation. He replied that he does not believe in nepotism. I asked what it meant, and he told me to look it up. I did and I've never forgotten that.

My father progressed from being a chief engineer to heading the entire electricity state organisation. Witnessing that was quite inspiring and I am sure I became an engineer because I was looking up to my dad.

In terms of internationally-known role models, Ratan Tata is a good choice. He chose a different route to grow and run an empire, and the company's management training and ethics training is world-class. I've met him a few times and he was inspiring.

I've also had great mentors in both companies I've worked for. Perhaps because it was during the division's formative business years, I was especially lucky with three mentors in a hierarchy during the early part of my career – my boss, his boss and his boss in turn. For some reason, I felt especially guided by my mentors. I think taking the time for people is an important part of leadership.

> THE IDEA: Nepotism and overt favouritism can be
> the bane of growth and independence and can also
> discourage other staff from performing at their best.

What did they mentor you in that in turn became the foundations for you as a leader?

I think they exercised discipline, transparency and clarity. They were very humorous and very human despite being highly respected. They knew their staff and I think that was the key. Although it was not always necessary, they knew a lot about the business. They also took the time to engage with people directly. When the opportunity in China emerged, I was actually supposed to head to the UK, which I wasn't particularly pleased about. Because of the engagement I had with my boss' boss, he remembered that I had an interest in Asia. He came to me directly and asked me if I would take on the role in China. That was very impressive to me – not because I was flattered, but because of his knowledge and awareness of the people in his team.

> THE IDEA: Having step-level (i.e. going beyond your
> direct subordinates) meetings with junior talents
> will not only help to inspire them, but also give
> you new insights that you may not get from direct
> subordinates.

What are some guiding principles that you live by?

I tend to focus on three year horizons. Obviously it Is important to recognise longer timeframes when developing braoder strategies. I first look at myself – what I can influence and what I'm paid to do, and then determine where the company needs to be in three years, and what is needed from the team to get to that point. I tend to have a goal, and then go into more details as I move into shorter term or specific goal. I think in three-year chunks, have a clear goal, and look at how my behaviour can drive the company and our people towards this goal.

Our company focuses on three themes from a behavioural perspective – winning right, communicating often and simply, and focusing together on the result. They're fairly specific and not all-encompassing. These match with what I believe drives success and with what has driven success. Things like personal engagement and walking around are important – if I'm in the office, I do not use the telephone to call someone, I walk over to their office. If they're not there, I benefit from just walking there and meeting other people along the way.

> THE IDEA: Change curves are getting shorter. Think
> in three-year chunks, formulate clear goals and
> look for behaviours that would drive the company
> and your people towards these goals.

Do you have advice on how to manage one's energy and work–life balance?

When entering a career, it is important to recognise that it is a long-haul journey and that work-life balance is important, although you have to be flexible in managing that balance. Things tend to happen in cycles or phases. Sometimes the work side of things needs extended focus, for example during strategic sales campaigns. It is never going to be an equal distribution all the time and there will be times when the balance consists of only work. Be aware of this and make choices that allow for it. I think technology today allows for greater work-life balance and society also has an expectation of work-life balance that did not exist in the past when priorities were different. How do you manage this balance while pursuing the leadership aspirations, success, drive, productivity and bandwidth you need to succeed and to rise to the top?

I made a decision very early on in my life not to work on the weekends. Of course I've worked during the weekends sometimes, but I generally don't, even during the early part of my career. I've tried not to bring work home. I try to be disciplined with respect to downtime.

> THE IDEA: There is no clear rule on how to achieve work-life balance albeit it clearly being important. Recognise the periods where you have to focus on the 'work' without the 'life', but ensure that you make up for it after the busy period is over.

LEADING OTHERS

In your opinion, is there a difference between managing and leading?

Managing is a subset of leading – I see management as an experience and skillset that allows you to lead, and think management training is important. If you are not a good manager, you would have less time to be a leader. As you progress, I think the management portion decreases and the leadership component increases. I admire companies that progressively place less emphasis on senior executives meeting business goals and instead focusing on them meeting leadership competencies. For organisations to groom better leaders, remuneration systems should be different. Leaders should be rewarded based on whether they have met competencies such as whether they have been a good leader, how many other leaders they have identified and supported within the organisation, and the morale level of the team.

> THE IDEA: If you do not manage well, you will have less time to lead.

What makes a good leader?

Having the ability to communicate and inspire, with a clear vision of an achievable yet challenging goal and being able to communicate it well. In addition, beyond managing in the administrative sense, being able to enqaqe your team and coaching are important skills. Choosing the right people is also an important atribute. A good leader's role is more akin to being 'first among equals' than adhering to a hierarchical structure, although clear structures are always helpful.

How do you choose people in your team? What do you look for and how do you groom them?

You can list some essential competencies, experience and success measures, which lowers the risk when choosing a person. When we select and interview someone, we have a process that allows us to bring out the key attributes we need to ascertain, the thinking we need to be aware of, the type of person that we are employing and the cultural fit in both directions. Cultural fit is most important for our customers, as well as for our company. Instinct also plays a big role when it comes to choosing a person, I don't know how to describe it otherwise.

> THE IDEA: When choosing new members for your team, beyond listing the necessary competencies, experience and success measures, listening to your instincts and determining cultural fit are also important criteria.

What sort of questions will you ask to test your instincts?

I ask completely irrelevant questions that are not necessarily personal. An example would be "how do you see the development of Singapore?" without explaining what I mean. Another example would be "what do you think about what's going on in Venezuela?" Some people might ask for guidance with the question and some might say that they do not know much about Venezuela, and that could be an absolutely perfect answer! These questions are less relevant to the role and often unexpected but they allow me to get to know the person because there are a lot of ways to say you don't know.

THE IDEA: Throwing a curve ball during the
interview session can be a good way of testing your
instincts and assessing the candidate based on
their responses.

LEADING THE ORGANISATION

Is there a leadership story in which you actualised your leadership philosophy by overcoming a business challenge?

We've grown tremendously in Singapore and added a lot of breadth and depth to what we do, which required considerable change management. We have shifted some important decision-making to this region, which was previously seen as a challenge to the existing management at the company headquarters. Through these transitions, I had to constantly communicate the leadership path we had to take as a company and manage difficult decisions such as those concerning restructuring. One of the most challenging management skills for me was getting the team to agree on a consistent approach in a complex situation.

The process of establishing our Seletar campus from a spark of an idea to convincing the decision-makers to take it seriously, to partnering the government and finally driving that through was an amazing experience. When I visit the Seletar Campus now, I'm still struck by how far we've come.

What else is in your leadership remit?

A big part of my job is identifying a particular geographical region's strategy, capability and intent over a long period of time, and what the decision will be in the future. These would then be mapped against any gaps in our capability and against our own challenges as a company. We also have to get the right people together to recognise these challenges and then decide how to tackle them. In short, getting the right people together to do the right thing.

What kind of challenges do you foresee in the future?

There is always the challenge of cost that goes hand in hand with the challenge to innovate and improve. Where the aerospace component of our industry is concerned, we invest a big chunk of our revenue in technology and capability, which drives efficiency and emission reductions every year. The nature of our business requires constant innovation and improvement in the efficiency of our equipment. In tangible terms, for example, this represents an improvement of about a percentage point in efficiency for each year of investment in technical development of our aero gas turbines. The challenge is to do that while reducing costs for our customer and we do so by increasingly identifying new opportunities where we can do that more effectively.

We expect to grow strongly over the next decade based on our substantial firm orderbook. As we continue to expand and as decision-making transfers from global to local networks, the search for talent and the right people continues to be one of the key challenge we face.

How are you tackling these challenges?

One of the approaches is to find new geographies to support our cost reduction programmes, such as looking at production in non-traditional locations. In terms of being able to deliver, it's an everyday focus on productivity, compliance and work ethics, driven by good leadership.

Another approach is to constantly fuel the talent pipeline. Long-term careers in our business are the norm, which can sometimes be a challenge to sell to young engineers in Asia. Hence we focus very strongly on raising the awareness of the benefits of the career, as well as all levels of people training and development. Our recruitment and selection process involves ensuring that our candidates understand that they have to gain experience before progressing to the next level of responsibility and authority.

Do you think there's a difference in leading a global organisation in Asia versus doing global work outside of Asia?

Cultural awareness is a key factor to succeeding in global organisations, and we're looking for local leaders that bring that with them, who do not think that it is necessary to adopt the "mother ship" culture in order to succeed in our company. Challenge is healthy and we encourage it. It takes courage not to emulate the cultures that are perceived as embedded in an MNC that has a non-Asian heritage. It is sometimes essential to recognise aspects of culture while not being a slave to it. Some of those cultures are essential, some are positive no matter where you are in the world, some of them belong in the geography that they are in and others do not belong at all. When operating in other cultures, such as in Asia, we want to infuse Asian culture with our core values and, at the same time, de-emphasize parts of our existing culture that are redundant. One of the most positive aspects of our company culture is our engineering discipline, which is universal regardless of the geographies we operate in.

THE IDEA: To lead in global organisations, respecting diversity and being able to adopt new disciplines and cultural behaviours in the way you work bodes well for success. Never feel that you need to fully adopt "mother ship" culture in order to blend in with the majority.

When you moved to Asia, how did you have to adapt in terms of your leadership style to be an effective leader?

I underwent the best training course I have ever experienced very early on in my career. It was a sales course, but it was really about people. One of the major facets of this was the importance of listening. In ones' own culture, it's easy to make assumptions and you are normally right. This is dangerous because your assumptions may not be right, but you take shortcuts because you know the culture and the way communication is understood in general. The way we communicate in another culture often needs to be different, not only becausee of possible language barriers. Listen to the last "drop" and make sure you really understand, and repeat it with clarity.

> THE IDEA: Listening is a fundamental leadership skill that builds understanding and trust. Always check for understanding and paraphrase to make sure that both parties see the same side of the story.

What is your advice for young leaders who are looking to work in other geographies?

I think you have to want it. We expect all leaders to want this kind of exposure to new geographies. If you want it, you need the drive to do it.

The economies of the world have evolved such that more Western organisations have ventured abroad in as compared to in the other direction. Historically, when Asian businesses have ventured overseas, as in the case of the Japanese, they have been extremely successful but may not have adapted in the way that some of their Western counterparts have. There is a difference in approach and the level of experience. In Asia there seems to be some level of inertia with regards to venturing abroad but we encourage people to work in different places. This experience is essential to becoming a global leader.

> THE IDEA: Do not wait for management to tap you on the shoulder to consider moving to new work geographies.

What legacy do you want to leave behind in Rolls-Royce?

For the first time, we now have a main board member from Asia, and it happens to be someone from Singapore. In addition I would expect to see at least two more representatives from Asia among the top leadership team of around ten. That would represent success in my book. Seats at the decision table from within this vibrant and fast growing region.

> THE IDEA: Aside from building the business, senior leaders should also focus on efforts to build the talent pipeline and help their leaders progress.

What final advice do you have for young leaders who want to succeed in the aerospace industry?

The complexity of what we do in the aerospace industry and the intricacy of the products that we produce and support are fascinating. They are entering an industry linked to GDP growth and especially growth of the middle class in the air travel segment. The growth in this region will be the highest and there is certainly a future in it. It's an industry to be proud of; I can't think of a person who would not feel pride at building part of an aeroplane or providing services related to it.

My advice for young leaders wanting to be a part of the industry would be to study hard because we choose the best. I understand that the entry requirement for aerospace degrees in Singapore is higher than for medicine. That tells you something about the industry and Singapore's focus on it. Learn about the industry, meet people in it and identify mentors. Understand that patience will be required and make that a virtue – drive with patience. Once you get to the senior positions, you are extremely valuable. We "force" our top graduate entrants to change their roles over the first few years, but they should then stick to one substanive role for three to five years in order to have real delivery experience and add value to themselves.

ALAN CHAN
Chief Executive Officer
Singapore Press Holdings (SPH)

BEING THE GAME-CHANGER

ALAN CHAN joined SPH as its Group President in July 2002, and was appointed Chief Executive Officer in January 2003. He is responsible for managing the group's portfolio of businesses, which includes newspapers, magazines and book publishing, Internet and mobile, broadcasting, events and out-ofhome advertising and properties.

Alan is on the boards of Singapore Press Holdings Ltd and its subsidiaries, including SPH REIT Management Pte Ltd; MediaCorp TV Holdings Pte Ltd and MediaCorp Press Ltd as well as Pavilion Energy Pte Ltd and Pavilion Gas Pte Ltd.

He currently chairs the External Review Panel for SAF Safety and the Singapore-China Foundation.

He is also a member of the Public Service Commission (PSC) and the Singapore Symphony Orchestra Council, and a director of Business China. He serves on the boards of the Federation Internationale of Periodics Publishers and the World Association of Newspapers and News Publishers (WAN-IFRA). He chaired the Council that revised the Code of Corporate Governance in 2012. He was also the Chairman of URA from 2006 to 2012.

Before joining SPH, Alan was an administrative officer in the civil service. He has worked in the government for 25 years and some of his previous appointments included Permanent Secretary of the Ministry of Transport, Deputy Secretary of the Ministry of Foreign Affairs, Principal Private Secretary to Senior Minister Lee Kuan Yew and Director of Manpower, Ministry of Defence.

Alan holds a Diplome d'Ingenieur from France's Ecole Nationale de l'Aviation Civile and an MBA (with Distinction) from INSEAD. He is a President's Scholar and was conferred the Public Administration Medal (Gold and Silver) and Meritorious Service Medal for his contributions to public service. In 2009, he was selected by INSEAD as "one of 50 Alumni who changed the world"

LEADING YOURSELF

What were some of the leadership transitions you undertook to become the CEO of Singapore Press Holdings?

I was very fortunate to win a French government scholarship at the age of 18 and was in the first batch of Singaporeans to study engineering in France. When I returned to Singapore at age 25, I served three years of National Service (NS) in the air force. In those days, it was two and a half years of NS plus six months of secondment. I was given the opportunity to undertake many key projects because at the time, there were only two graduates in the HQ Republic of Singapore Air Force (RSAF) Air Operations Department.

When I finished my NS, I joined the Department of Civil Aviation and was part of the team that developed Changi Airport. On my first day of work, I was made the manager of Seletar Airport. The airport was handed to me after just two hours of briefing. Because of my university training and my three years in the air force, I knew exactly what to do with the airport. While serving in Changi Airport, I was offered another scholarship and went to INSEAD for my MBA. Upon my return, I was asked to switch to administrative service. I went through the Ministry of Home Affairs and Ministry of Defence, before serving as the Principal Private Secretary to Mr Lee Kuan Yew. Subsequently, I served in the Ministry of Foreign Affairs, Ministry of Communications and Information Technology and then the Ministry of Transport.

At the age of 49, I was offered the helm of SPH by Mr Lim Kim San, who was then the Executive Chairman. That was how I ended up in SPH, and it has been 12 years since then.

Who are some of the leadership role models you encountered that gave you a semblance of what you should be like as a leader?

Because I started work in the late 1970s, the impact of the first generation leadership was very strong. I was fortunate to work under BG(Retd) Tan Chin Tiong, who was then the Permanent Secretary for the Ministry of Home Affairs, and who had served with Dr Goh Keng Swee. The things that he learnt from Dr Goh were passed on to me. And of course, I worked under Mr Lee Kuan Yew himself for three years. I think the virtues and thoroughness of the first generation leadership rubbed off on me and became second nature.

Were there specific stories or things that you learnt from them that impacted you now?

There was a lot of wisdom on why we did various things. With the Ministry of Defence, for example, there was a desire for civilian control. Whether it was the Permanent Secretary, the Director of Finance, Manpower or Logistics, they were civil service and not military appointments. The fact that many key MINDEF leaders were civil servants gave the public the assurance that their NS sons had a neutral party to turn to.

When I went on foreign trips with Mr Lee Kuan Yew, he made it a point to visit the local markets because this would tell him what was available in the country, and if it was prosperous. He would also check on the price of an egg and ask about the salaries of the locals. In those days when we worked on Saturdays, he would ask me at short notice to visit a certain precinct in the afternoon. He would ask to visit a couple of families and enquire about the cost of living and how the families were getting on. There was a lot of first-hand experience.

> THE IDEA: Being accessible and visible as a leader goes a long way to demonstrate that you understand the issues on the ground and are thus not making up policies merely from the ivory tower.

I used to work for Mr Sim Kee Boon, the former head of Civil Service and Permanent Secretary for the Ministry of Communications. His most memorable instruction to us in Changi Airport was "not a single broken tile". He would not tolerate a single broken tile, and this simple concept applied to everything from the baggage system to the computer check-in system. He would not accept any flaws, and this simple instruction was immediately understood by everyone in the organisation. It was a simple but effective message.

These are the sort of strong leadership lessons I've learnt in my career, and up till today, I still try to practise them.

> THE IDEA: Refusing to allow minor flaws in your area of leadership helps to ensure that you and your team do not slip into apathy.

What are some leadership principles that you have lived by since you were a young executive?

Delegation. I learnt to do so the hard way, and I still see it not being practised enough by my young executives. Many good executives want to do everything themselves. I was also guilty of this when I was younger. At the Ministry of Home Affairs, I was in charge of four departments and I rewrote every paper prepared by my department heads. I wanted to ensure that they were of an "A" standard. But when I went to the Ministry of Defence, I was put in charge of 11 departments and almost collapsed trying to rewrite all their submissions. It was impossible to redo everything, and that was when I learnt to delegate authority and to accept a "B" piece of work. You cannot expect an "A" piece of work from everybody. One important lesson I learnt in the Ministry of Defence was "do not analyse to paralyse".

> THE IDEA: Having a lot of responsibilities on your plate can be a very daunting task. Delegate, but be conscious of areas that require you to focus on the details and do not overanalyse less significant issues.

What gets you out of bed every day?

The good thing about working in the newspaper business is that each day brings about fresh excitement. There seems to be something exciting happening every day, and we get to hear the inside story first. To me, life is lived through the newspaper, and I think that being in a news organisation is one of the best jobs anyone can hope for.

With so many conflicting priorities, what tips have you have learnt on your journey in life? How do you manage your energy and time and work–life balance?

As I mentioned earlier, I tried doing everything myself and almost collapsed. You need to prioritise your work and not chase everything. However, I feel sad when I see some people in notable positions who do not have a vision or sense of purpose. I like to call this the "missionary zeal". If you are running an educational institution, the aim is not just to produce graduates with technical skills. You should transform the students and help them aim for greater heights. This is the missionary zeal that I'm talking about – every leader must have some.

Many colleagues just like to do the same thing day after day. However, for a colleague to distinguish himself, he has to be a game-changer. Someone who can think out of the ordinary and accomplish big things for the organisation. For many years, we were struggling with our radio business. Suddenly, a game-changer brought in the right combination of people and music and transformed the radio stations. Overnight, we were the most listened-to radio station in Singapore, and the profits started rolling in. I hope this can be replicated in other parts of the organisation.

THE IDEA: Approach your work with a sense of missionary zeal. Look beyond the day-to-day routine and seek to find the greater purpose of why your team and organisation exists. Look for game-changers in the organisation and work closely with them to achieve your goals.

What do you look for in a game-changer?

A game-changer is not someone who continues with the way things have always been done. He is someone who is prepared to experiment and try new ideas and bring about a buzz in the organisation.

THE IDEA: Dare to be a game-changer and experiment and try new things.

What makes you a good leader?

During a lunch meet-up with my ex colleagues from the Ministry of Foreign Affairs (MFA), I told them that I regretted spending only two short years at the Ministry. One of them replied, "Mr Chan, your two years were enough to leave an impression on all of us. Even now, 12 to 15 years later, we still come back to look for you. You have always been our friend and a mentor."

In MFA, everyone is a specialist, and I was parachuted in overnight as the Deputy Secretary. There was only one thing expected of me – to help them to do their jobs better. If I couldn't help them, I would be useless. To be successful, I needed to help my subordinates to grow.

One of the best lessons I've learnt was from Akio Morita, the co-founder of Sony. At his zenith, he promoted people on the basis of the number of managers the person was able to nurture and produce. If he had two senior managers, and one of them nurtured two subordinates to run South America and the stereo section, while the other senior manager did not nurture any one, the first would be richly rewarded. Being able to produce good managers for the organisation was to ensure its continuity and survival.

> THE IDEA: Your job as a leader is to help others do their job better and to look for opportunities to produce new leaders.

You are very used to jettisoning into a leadership position, but not completely used to being a content or organisational expert. During the first three months of taking on a new position, what do you do to make sure you are adding value?

Two things are important: education and constant learning. I went to a French Grande École, which was very different from the Anglo-Saxon university model. The French view is that if you can get into the Grande École, you are smart enough. They will give the student the widest exposure in numerous subjects. In a typical year, I would study 30 subjects ranging from aerodynamics to work psychology. We were tested on four major projects each year, where we needed to make use of the 30 subjects learnt. In this diverse world, you need to have an understanding of many subjects. More importantly, you need to keep up to date as knowledge evolves rapidly. One has to read and attend seminars regularly to remain ahead.

LEADING OTHERS

What do you look for when you build an effective team? How do you groom your leaders as you build an organisation?

Obviously, you have to make sure that the person whom you've picked can do the job. If he can't do it, you have to look for a way for him to exit.

Having formed your team, socialisation is key. In SPH, my direct subordinates and I bet on trivialities such as how many medals Singapore will win at the Asian Games, with the loser having to buy dinner. After a few betting dinners, people get to know one another better. It is a way to build up camaraderie in an informal setting. The different divisions in SPH take turns to organise a monthly "happy hour" event where there is free beer and food. This is to promote socialising among the various divisions. I learnt this principle from the military officer mess and from the MFA, which has a monthly "chardonnay hour". Socialising in an informal setting facilitates work coordination among colleagues with less confrontations.

> THE IDEA: Socialising and injecting an element of friendly competition among team members helps to integrate new members and build camaraderie.

Please share your experience of a leadership challenge that you had to overcome.

When I joined SPH in 2002, it was two years after the liberalisation of the media sector. SPH used to run a TV station called *MediaWorks*. At the same time, MediaCorp Pte Ltd started a newspaper called

Today. There was intense competition, with both companies losing hundreds of millions of dollars. One of my first missions was to stop the bleeding. It took more than two years for me to negotiate a merger with Ernest Wong, the CEO of MediaCorp. There were times when we wanted to give up, but we persevered. Eventually, we negotiated a merger between MediaWorks and MediaCorp. Currently, SPH owns 20% of MediaCorp TV. SPH's *Streats* newspaper was merged with *Today*, with SPH owning a 40% share. I've stopped the bleeding and brought sensible competition to the media industry.

What have you learnt from your experience as a leader?

The biggest challenge was to persuade the authorities that media competition and liberalisation were not sustainable in Singapore. In the TV industry, the highest bidder would get the programme from the Hollywood or Hong Kong studios. However, we might not earn sufficient revenue to cover the contracted price due to our small market. We used a step-by-step approach to explain the intricacies to the civil servants and ministers.

My colleagues wanted to give up on the merger negotiations several times, but giving up wasn't a solution – it meant many more years of bleeding. At one stage, the discussions got so heated that Ernest and I decided to call things to a halt. We stopped negotiations and cooled down before meeting again after two months and ploughed on until we reached an agreement.

Another thing was minimising job losses. We wanted to make sure that there was no victimisation and decided to get neutral board members to chair the HR process. These processes required a lot of perseverance.

> THE IDEA: Perseverance is key as a leader. Do not walk away from dealing with important issues and instead take a step back and revisit these issues when emotions subside.

LEADING THE ORGANISATION

What is your vision for SPH?

SPH traces its history back to 1845 when the first copy of *The Straits Times* was published. My vision for SPH is for it to remain a major news source for Singaporeans, be it via newspapers or other modern media platforms, and to diversify into sufficient new areas to remain a blue chip stock.

What are some of the highlights over these 12 years of leading SPH?

As you know, the newspaper industry is a mature one. The younger generations are moving to other mediums such as the Internet, tablets and smartphones. It is a big challenge for the company and we need to build other growth areas. I am quite pleased with the following three areas:

When I joined SPH, it had five magazines with a turnover of $20 million. Today, we have grown the magazine sector to about 120 magazines with a turnover of $100 million spread over Southeast Asia, China and India. It was something that we built over the years and we are proud of it.

Back then, we had bought Paragon and were redeveloping it. The Board also decided to sell the Straits Times site in Kim Seng Road instead of developing it on our own. When Dr Tony Tan came on board as our chairman, he threw me the challenge of building a property arm in SPH. So we built the luxury condominium, Sky @ Eleven, using our warehouse land. This was sold out in 30 hours. We took part in a public tender and won the bid for Clementi Mall. With Paragon and Clementi Mall, we created the SPH REIT and enhanced value for our shareholders. We also won the bid for Seletar Mall, which we are currently developing.

Lastly, we created an exhibition arm and bought over the COMEX and IT shows. Our exhibitions and shows are now in Singapore, Malaysia, Indonesia and Myanmar. Very soon, we'll be starting the next set of shows in Vietnam and in the Philippines. We are hoping to replicate what the magazines have done in the exhibitions area. All these were built from scratch over the last five years.

As part of my approach, I have always used a project sponsor from within the company. I give my direct subordinates a chance to unleash their entrepreneurial talent and build a business. If I had just bought a business with an external team, the internal staff would not care as it has nothing to do with them. Now that they have a stake in it, they have an interest to make the business successful.

> THE IDEA: A leader always looks out for new opportunities to expand and aims to source internally within his/her team to branch them out to these opportunities..

Who are SPH's key competitors?

In the old days, we had a monopoly in the newspaper business but that is no longer the case now. Our current competitors include mobiles and the Internet. Not only do we have competition from foreign newspapers, social media and news sites such as the

BBC, we also have competition in the advertising sphere. In the past, advertising mostly involved simple banners, but today, our competitors are Google, Facebook and Twitter, because they also run advertisements. If you are an advertiser, you would go to a medium that is most effective. The entire media sphere is now our competitor and it is getting tougher.

How do you cope with this competition?

SPH's strength lies in local news. It is through attracting local eyeballs that we serve the advertisers. In addition, we now have an all-in-one package for a certain price, where users have access to the physical and Internet version of our newspapers as well as access on four mobile devices. These four devices can be shared among one's spouse, siblings and children.

We live in a volatile, uncertain, complex and ambiguous (VUCA) world. What is your vision for leading SPH through these situations? How do you intend to become good-to-great or great-to-greater?

Colleagues must share the same vision. I do not profess to know everything. It is for the younger and more up-to-date staff to come up with ideas; I can only provide them with wisdom and evaluate the feasibility of their ideas.

We have just come up with two initiatives in SPH. First, we have an idea incubator. If a staff's idea passes the review committee, the staff is given up to 100 days and a grant of $30,000 to develop it. Second, we have created a $100 million fund to invest into new start-ups. Even if just one project succeeds out of the many we invest in, if this project can bring in $200 million, I will have succeeded. This is the change in mindset that we need. We want the staff to feel valued, but they also have to prove themselves.

What do you look for in SPH scholars?

There are two types of scholarships. One is in journalism, where the scholars become journalists who write and edit articles. The other is the management scholarship. However, some of my best staff are non-scholars from local universities. The scholarship is sometimes overhyped. Frankly, you don't need to be a scholar to be capable. You can be a normal Joe and yet turn out to be a marvellous leader or manager so long as you have the drive and EQ.

Many people say that Singaporeans tend not to be as ready to take on leadership roles, and often pale in comparison to foreigners. What do you think is needed to groom local leaders in organisations?

My biggest regret is that I've never worked outside of Singapore despite being trilingual. I would encourage the younger generation to go abroad. In the past, people look at overseas postings as good opportunities to make money, where they look for compensations in areas such as overseas allowances, transport and lodging. It is time to shed such thinking as salaries in Singapore are already very attractive even when compared to developed countries. If you are a young and budding executive wanting to build a portfolio, being calculative does not help. The experience of an overseas posting can completely transform a person. In addition, don't be choosy. Working in challenging environments such as Yangon or Jakarta will shorten the learning curve much faster than in comfortable western cities.

Many people want to go for glamourous high-flying careers. For ten years, I was in Finance and HR departments instead of Policy and Operations postings. While they may appear boring, I learnt a lot about resource allocation and control. I've done HR, procurement, administration and finance, and also managed 200 tenancies in Seletar Airport. I think that gave me a very different perspective.

> THE IDEA: Getting your reins as a leader is far
> easier if you get your hands dirty at some point in
> your career.

What are your current priorities in leading SPH now?

Now that I am nearing my retirement, my priority is to plan for succession. I want to have business units that can operate on their own and I give a lot of flexibility to my direct subordinates. It does not mean that I am not watching over them; I point it out to them when they are doing something wrong, and I praise them when they are doing well. For people on the ground, a simple email of praise from the boss goes a long way. In the early days, when a lot of engineers were made admin officers, Mr Lee Kuan Yew was not satisfied with the standard of written English. When we put up papers to the Cabinet, it had to first pass through a Permanent Secretary. When I received praise for "good analysis" from Mr J. Y. Pillay for a paper on community policing, I felt like I was in seventh heaven.

> THE IDEA: Never be stingy with your praise when it
> is due. Cultivate the habit of catching people doing
> the "right" thing and not just the "wrong".

When you retire, what is the legacy you wish to leave behind for future young leaders?

I hope to be remembered as a person who kept the SPH flag flying and built a series of growth sectors for the company while producing high quality news for the country.

What are your plans after retirement?

I am essentially a Western-educated person as I went to English schools and French universities. I've always felt a gap in my life from not knowing enough about Chinese culture and history. One of my ambitions is to read the entire set of *The Cambridge History of China* when I retire.

PHYLLIS CHEUNG
Managing Director
McDonald's China

BE AUTHENTIC AND STAND FOR SOMETHING

PHYLLIS CHEUNG was Managing Director of McDonald's Singapore from 2012 to mid 2014. Prior to her Singapore stint, she was Vice President and General Manager of McDonald's China South Region, and was responsible for the accelerated restaurant openings, people development and operation management of more than 550 restaurants.

Before Phyllis changed her career path to line management, she was the Vice President and Chief Marketing Officer of McDonald's China, where she was instrumental in driving business growth and spearheading commercial, product and new business initiatives, while also championing talent development.

Shortly after this interview was completed, Phyllis relocated back to China. She is now Managing Director of McDonald's China, responsible for the market's penetration, brand and organisational development strategy. McDonald's China today operates over 2,000 restaurants and employs over 100,000 employees.

LEADING YOURSELF

How did you progress from starting your career post graduation to becoming the Managing Director of McDonald's?

When I first started working, I never thought about how far I should go – I just kept going. I think the first start is finding something that I really love to do. My first degree was actually in music and comparative literature but I was also very interested in the commercial world and hence tried to find a bridge between creativity and commercialism in my career pursuit.

I found it in the world of advertising, which was my first career for eight years. It was an exhilarating start during the Asian financial crisis and I was promoted very quickly to a Brand Director at the age of 27.

How did success taste like at such a young age?

It tasted sweet only for a short while. During the Asian financial crisis, I suddenly found myself inadequate as the clients did not buy most of the solutions that I had proposed. I felt the need to think more strategically and took the opportunity to work with my mentor at his brand consultancy in India in the late 1990s. As a consultant, I was able to listen to the conversations in the boardroom, which was a great lesson for me in separating theory from practical management. In theory, leadership needs to take care of the company vision and the strategic decisions but in reality, a lot of decisions are made after considering a breadth of constraints and the dynamics of the teams and organisational capabilities. In order to lead and influence the entire leadership team to take certain directions, you require not just professional skill but also organisational leadership skill.

> THE IDEA: At a certain point in your leadership transitions, you may feel out of depth and that would be a good time to engage an external consultant or executive coach to guide you through these transitions.

How did you join Mcdonald's?

After I returned from India, I made a career choice to switch from consultancy to client so that I can be in charge of the end-to-end strategy to execution. I also made a point about wanting to join a people-oriented organisation where people are the brand-builders. In 2000, I had the opportunity to work for McDonald's and started as an Assistant Marketing Manager. My salary was lower as I did not have the required experience, but I was okay with it because I had the chance to change fields. The first transition is realising how interested you are in making a difference. In a leadership role, you have a lot of drive to make things happen. The second realisation is that you really have to be at the top to make a difference. While I was at marketing, my dream job was to become the Chief Marketing Officer of McDonald's. You have a budget and there are a lot of things you can do and many ideas that you can actualise. Shortly after attaining that role, I realised that you need to be a Managing Director in order to make a holistic and sustainable impact.

How did you go from an Assistant Manager to the Managing Director?

The path was never easy. The first years were more focused on leading yourself, you did not necessarily get a lot of coaching from others, but you learned by making a lot of mistakes and in working collaboratively with others.

As a junior, your goal is to achieve results – and to be seen and recognised. At mid-management level, it is very important to build your network of influence. I think this is where I have an advantage; I didn't realise how much I had learnt at the mid-management level during my years in advertising. I was able to energize the cross functional team towards finding a solution to a challenge.

I was only promoted to director level after five years. But I took off very quickly because I understood how to motivate the frontline and the critical success factors to execution excellence. Within two years, I was promoted to Chief Marketing Officer because of my forte in strategic planning and capability to turn strategy into execution. Then, my boss suggested to me one day that I should consider changing path to do line management. I jumped on that opportunity right away. It was very slow at the beginning, but once you get the opportunity, you suddenly accelerate.

THE IDEA: The early foundations you lay as a leader in a new role and organisation are crucial to your survival and promotion. Prove your worth with the results you deliver, and build your network of influence and know the organisation front to back!

Did you have any role models while you were growing up? What did you learn from them?

At the mid-management level, you definitely look up to role models. What I did was to look within the region to find business leaders whom I really aspired to be like and noted what their strengths were. I read their work and observed how they strategised. I cannot name a specific role model, but I try to learn from the different leaders and their strengths to make them my own.

Sitting in meetings also allowed me to observe how leaders facilitate conversation and how they bring out the best value of the other top talents in the organisation. I did a lot of observational learning when I was at the mid-management level.

> THE IDEA: Observe role models, especially in senior boardroom meetings and townhalls, to pick up on the best practices in strategising and decision making.

What are some of the best things that you learnt from these observations?

I think the first thing is to provide clarity on what the issues and endings are. In leading a high performing leadership team, what you need to provide is clarity of purpose – what are we trying to achieve as a bigger and more ambitious goal? Everything becomes clearer from there. The tactics or strategies employed can be different, but once you elevate the conversation to a higher level, everyone will be much more excited and the conversation would be far more stimulating. The team will start to focus on finding the best scenario to approach an issue rather than being restricted to certain pre-concluded recommendations.

The second thing is listening for value. Some of the CEOs that I worked with are not necessarily the best strategists in the organisation, but they do well because they listen actively and are able to extract value by listening to people. During this process, the best strategic thinking will emerge. Never work on your own strategy by closing the door. At McDonald's, one of the most popular quotes from our founder Ray Kroc is "None of us is as good as all of us". Collective wisdom can always make things better. It's important to engage your leadership team in charting the company's future so that everyone owns the strategy, they believe in it and they are all committed to it.

> THE IDEA: In order to engage all stakeholders to take action on ambitious goals, leaders need to provide clarity on how these goals connect to the overall strategy and take time to listen to all relevant concerns. Ultimately, the decisions may not please everyone but all stakeholders should feel that they were consulted

With almost 20 years of experience in leading others, what are some key leadership principles that you live by?

As a leader, you need to provide clarity of purpose and direction to the team. At the same time, you have to empower the team to explore solutions by themselves rather than mandating them or guiding them to a solution that you have experience with. Empowerment itself is very motivational. That is getting the best out of your team.

Another principle is to be honest, fair and consistent. As a leader, people take what you say very seriously. Think through what you want to do and identify the top three things to focus on. Provide that focus repeatedly and consistently so that people people will not drift or be swayed by day-to-day operational nuisance.

One more principle is to make time for future thinking and innovation. You have to set aside resources and time for exploration and building the future. On a day-to-day basis, however, you have to be very focused on your top three things, you need to drive both short-term results and long-term vision plan.

> THE IDEA: As a leader, your actions and words are under constant scrutiny and will be interpreted and sometimes misinterpreted. Being consistent and keeping your focus to a few key agenda will help to align your team towards effective execution.

How do you manage your time and energy on a day-to-day basis?

I am a workaholic, and do not have a normal work-life balance. I try to manage by making sure that I have my me-time and reflection time. Look at your calendar constantly – have you scheduled the most important thing? You need to make sure you prioritise your time very well.

Reflection time is important because my scheulde is usually packed with meetings and travels. Setting aside reflection time allows me to clear my head to consolidate my thoughts. I challenge myself often in these reflection time about what could I have done differently to lead towards a better outcome. It is through these reflection time that I become a better me, and a better leader.

> THE IDEA: Amid your busy schedule, take the time to reflect on your decisions. Taking 10 minutes to stare out of the window can be all it takes to broaden your strategic horizon.

When do you do your best reflection?

After the end of every day, I have at least 30 minutes to look at the notes that I've jotted down during the day especially the critical conversations I have had. I identify the issues and conflicts that happened during the day and develop different perspective, alternative scenarios or ideas towards resolving them.

LEADING OTHERS

What do you think the difference is between a good leader and a good manager?

Managing is basically being focused on executing goals. You manage a project, you manage a team. You make sure that goals are set, and decide on the key areas and scope of the project.

As a leader, you paint a future picture for your organisation, inspire the team and guide them towards realizing that dream. Being a leader means that you have a bigger view of the market and whole organisation, and whether resources are orchestrated towards the same goal. Your role is focused more on resourcing and enabling others.

> THE IDEA: Leaders have to take a step back from day-to-day execution to consider how the pieces fit together to form a bigger picture. They look into resourcing the projects and teams, always with a future perspective.

In your opinion, what makes the best leaders?

You need to be authentic about yourself and stand for something that can inspire people. A great leader is someone who is visionary. A lot of people have big ideas, but I think the perfect combination would be being both visionary and focused on building the organisation that lasts. A great leader left behind a legacy of core strengths, culture and values.

Please share a story demonstrating you at your best as a leader.

The most recent incident would be navigating the McDonald's Singapore organisation through the restructuring of Singapore's economy and the changing consumer landscape.

I spent a lot of time with the leadership team to articulate the issues and to paint our future picture. I think what I do best is to lead the team to anticipate changes, and be very energized by the idea of leading change.

Building your team as a new leader involves earning trust from your leadership team. The team experienced quite a couple of managing directors in the past and so felt that I would just be another 'stop & go' MD. What I did was to be authentic and to be honest about areas that I need help. During a team meeting two months after I had joined, I expressed my desire to earn the team's trust. The team shared their concerns and expectations, and I addressed them one by one. I showed my commitment and they also show theirs – and at the end of that meeting, we all signed a pledge. Be authentic about the situation and yourself and deliver on your commitments. Not only do we have a good working relationship in the leadership team now, we also have good friendships.

THE IDEA: As you lead a younger generation of millenials who do not respond as well to hierarchy and authoritarian styles of leadership, be authentic to your followers and cultivate friendships with them.

Is it easy to have friendships with your employees?

I was told that I don't need to like the person, and that all I needed was to have respect for and a professional relationship with him or her. But what I experienced is that you really need to enjoy working with your team. I feel that even if you don't have a good first impression of a person, you need to be positive and look at their good points. Leverage their strengths while being very constructive about their opportunities.

Some people may think that it is not professional to have too many emotional bonds, but I think a better way to describe it is to have "chemistry". We are human beings and we produce better work in an environment that we feel secured. In order to have good chemistry, you need to put energy into the team. The team should not just focus on competing – although a competitive spirit is important – but they should also help each other out. We don't necessarily have to be close friends, but we definitely need to be able to trust each other as work partners and enjoy working with one another.

The important thing is that you need to deliver on your expectations and do your performance review fairly and assertively. You need to have accountability and empathy on a personal and on a professional level. It's a fine line you have to draw.

> THE IDEA: Build a team that does not only compete within itself, and that has enough trust and camaraderie to look out for each other in order to compete with other industry players.

What do you look for when building a team?

Shared purpose and values. As a team, we all need to share the passion towards achieving a common purpose. Hiring people for the right attitude is more important than just their skills alone. While the team needs to have the right mix of skills, underlying this is having the right attitude that is in line with the organisation's values. Diversity is important. My team consists of 50% existing McDonald's employees and 50% new hires. This is important to have a balanced outside-in view of the company and at the same time adding new core competencies to strengthen the company's competitiveness towards winning the future..

> THE IDEA: Hire for the right skills, but more importantly, the right attitude.

You mentioned needing to build a circle of influence. Do you have any advice for people who are new in an organisation to build their networks in order to be successful?

Offer yourself as a resource to others. This is the easiest way as a junior level staff or those at a mid-management level. You create your demand. The new generation is a bit too calculative in terms of their job scope. This is the best time to learn, and you should expand your scope as much as possible – avoid being too calculative and offer yourself to others.

> THE IDEA: If you find yourself drawing too many lines to protect your job scope, you may soon be left out of the circle.

How does one offer himself as a resource?

Try to work with different departments in order to expand your network. Secondly, try to learn how others think and the perspectives of other departments. After understanding their perspectives, you can then work together to find a solution so people don't feel that you are just driving your own agenda.

What are some of the key reasons that some leaders fail?

It can be many reasons. One reason may be that they are unable to see a clear picture of where the business currently is and what the key issues are. When you are at the top, you probably have a lot of information, but how much of this information is telling you the truth and how much of it is just trying to make you feel better?

Another reason for failure could be a lack of engagement where leaders fail to make their team understand their goals.

It could also be a lack of capable people around you. You might have a lot of people who have been successful in the past, but they may not have the right skills to move forward. Have you been able to surround yourself with the right people at the right time?

> THE IDEA: Be careful of potential leadership derailers such as failing to make sense of issues and information to make informed decisions, a lack of engagement with team members and failure to build an effective team.

How does one manage their boss?

Communication. Tell a simple story of why, where and how. Why are you doing good or bad, where will you go next, and how will you get there. That's important because you need to gauge the support of the boss and that he or she being able to repeat your story to many others. It would be an ideal situation if your boss can become your advocate. Help your boss to be able to tell a good story, to sell the plan and get the right resources.

THE IDEA: Bringing your boss on board with you requires simplifying your why, where and how into a story that your boss can advocate and repeat to others to gain traction and commitment.

LEADING THE ORGANISATION

Tell me about the McDonald's organisation under your charge and the new role that you are moving to.

Organisational strategy is becoming increasingly important in helping a company's success. Our future success lies in the capability of the team to strategize and to execute. While one cannot 100% accurately predict the future, you can predict whether you have the capability and the capacity within your organisation to meet the challenges and hence focus on building these capabilities.

To that end, training leadership and development has become our core competence. We are the best in the industry, but we still have some room to do better. People see us as world class fast-food operators, but in order to attract top talent, we need to profile ourselves higher. We have just launched a leadership academy in September 2014 and aligned our training functions to be like an academy. How do we make education and training our core competence? It works both ways in terms of retention and recruitment. We have looked into this area to make it stronger.

Another important aspect that we are working on is technological capacity. We are very good at global innovations in the restaurants. However, we are not innovative enough in a consumer noticeable manner. We are importing technology and digital capability to the organisation in order to win the future.

How would you describe the organisation in Singapore right now?

We have 128 restaurants in Singapore. In terms of density, we have one restaurant for every 46,000 people – the third-highest density in Asia Pacific. We employ more than 8,900 employees – 60% are part-timers while 40% are full-timers. If we count alumni, 100,000 people in Singapore have worked in McDonald's once in their lifetime. We are one of the front innovators with the invention of McDelivery and in terms of volume and business, McDelivery is currently number one in the world. We drive the most transactions out of the McDelivery hub. Our business is 24/7 and breakfast items make up 20% of our daily sales, which means that we have more room to grow. We are also looking at new growth opportunities such as cafes, desserts and beverages. The fundamentals of our business are building on providing super convenience and accessible quality food to consumers. Moving forward, we want to evolve the business to not just be about convenience and price, but to be more experiential. That's why the strategies regarding people and technology for different experiential models are going to be important

What are the challenges you see in the McDonald's industry?

Consumers' changing lifestyle and perception about fast food. We have to make sure that we communicate and evolve our food to stay relevant to the consumers' needs. That's why we have new wholesome choices in addition to our Big Macs that people love.

Another challenge is the experiential aspect of the business. In the past, being very fast was a competitive advantage. But now, people want a more hassle-free experience. Instead of wanting fast service, they now look for simple, easy enjoyment.

The third challenge lies in how do we engage today's consumers in our brand's conversation? Consumers care more about authentic acts rather than ads.

What are you currently doing to cope with these challenges?

On an organisational level, we try to fill the gaps in the skills that we do not have and from a consumer engagement standpoint, we look at building our digital base and content.

In terms of lifestyle adaptation, we have identified what we want to achieve in one year and three years with regard to menu development. We are also collaborating with the Health Promotion Board to really understand what they are trying to achieve and be part of the solutions towards better eating.

How do you motivate people when you are not the market leader when it comes to wages?

What we've found through internal research is that pay is important to people, but not the most important factor. Wages can attract people to join the company, but after they have joined, satisfaction comes from working relationships, whether they like their jobs and opportunities to progress. We've found out that people like our fun environment and family elements, and being able to learn things that they cannot learn from other organisations. Students who join us get to experience a first taste of life and learn discipline, teamwork and about the business. For women who are just returning to the workforce, being able to contribute to the team gives them self-worth. In terms of career paths, you can progress to be a trainer if you are able to command all the stations. You can then subsequently be promoted to floor manager. Our strength lies in providing training across each career move. Because we are so transparent about the career paths, people do not feel stuck in one position.

> THE IDEA: You need to pay your employees enough
> for them not to worry about money issues, but
> beyond that, focus their energy towards building
> experiences, e.g. increasing their self-worth in doing
> meaningful work, having advancement/learning
> opportunities and working in positive environments.

What do you foresee in terms of differences and challenges when moving from a small market in Singapore to China?

The scale is very different. There are over 2,000 restaurants in China compared to 128 in Singapore. China's size and granularity of opportunities is comparable to the European Union. It's akin to managing a portfolio of markets and the focus would be more on strategies on an enterprise level. It's even more important that strategies are articulated clearly. There is also the challenge of how to disseminate what we are trying to achieve from the top to all the provinces and cities at the field. At the same time, we need to make sure that we train our people fast enough so that we can continue to accelerate our restaurant growth. In Singapore, you can go down to any restaurant to resolve a specific problem immediately, but in China, you wouldn't be able to do that, you need to rely on your local teams to do that. It's even more important to build your organisation with strong teams of shared purpose and values..

> THE IDEA: As your scope of responsibilities
> increases as a leader, you will need to articulate your
> strategies with greater clarity and focus on building
> capabilities within your team. Micro-management
> can never work in enterprise leadership.

What advice do you have for someone who wants to be a leader in the F&B industry?

You have to know what you want to stand for because there are so many competitors. What is your advantage? What do you want people to remember you for? What is your signature? It could be a dish or even your service.

In terms of coming up with a concept, people in Singapore are doing quite well. The next phase is how to scale your business. What would your scaling model be like? Building one or two restaurants is easy, but building many more restaurants with a consistent experience requires a focus on the system. I think many entrepreneurs are very good individual leaders, but they need a lot of help when it comes to building an organisation and system.

It is also important to think about how you are going to compete for the future. The retail industry will be significantly affected by online businesses. There is a lot of unchartered water ahead and I think the winning team will be the one who can successfully anticipate changes, figures out how to navigate it and what that future would be like.

> THE IDEA: Just like running a consumer brand, you need to think about your unique leadership signature (e.g. strengths, knowledge, style, personality etc.) and be consistent in the way you market your brand (e.g. grooming, communication, online presence etc.).

KOH POH TIONG
Chairman and Senior Advisor, Ezra Holdings
Board Member, Fraser and Neave Limited

LEADERS DO WELL BY DOING GOOD

KOH POH TIONG is currently the Chairman and Senior Advisor of Ezra Holdings Limited. He is also advisor to and a member of the Board of Fraser and Neave Limited. Mr Koh retired as CEO of Fraser and Neave Limited (Food & Beverage Division) in October 2011, having previously served as CEO of Asia Pacific Breweries from 1993 to 2008. He was appointed Non-Executive Chairman of Times Publishing Limited on 3 March 2014.

He continues to serve as a director at The Great Eastern Life Assurance Company Limited, SATS Ltd, United Engineers Limited, Petra Foods Limited and Raffles Medical Group. Mr Koh is currently the Chairman of the National Kidney Foundation and Council Chairman of The Singapore Kindness Movement. In addition, Mr Koh was also the Chairman of the Agri-Food & Veterinary Authority and Director at Wildlife

Reserves Singapore Pte Ltd, Jurong Bird Park Pte Ltd and Media
Corporation of Singapore Pte Ltd.

Mr Koh is noted for his strong civic involvement and long-
standing interest in sports and education. He has served on
the Singapore Youth Olympic Games Organising Committee,
the Singapore Sports Council and the Football Association of
Singapore, in addition to being Chairman of the Gan Eng Seng
School's Advisory Committee and on the MBA Advisory Board
of Nanyang Technological University. For his contributions to
society and business, Mr Koh was conferred both the Public
Service Medal and the Service to Education Medal in 2007. He
was also named Outstanding Chief Executive of the Year at
the Singapore Business Awards 1998 by DHL and *The Business
Times*. Mr Koh was conferred the Public Service Star Award
in October 2013 for his contributions as Chairman of the
Singapore Kindness Movement.

LEADING YOURSELF

What were some early life lessons that shaped your perspectives?

I started Primary 1 in 1954, and from the very beginning, my father
expected me to top the class every term. When I did not, I would
be punished, and he would refuse to sign my report card. The
pressure on me was immense, and I rebelled against him when I was
in secondary school. I lost interest in my studies, formed two pop
bands, participated in most of the school's extra-curricular activities
and deliberately returned home late most of the time.

Then one of the best things happened – I became the worst
performer in Secondary 3. I was ranked 44 out of 44 students! I
vividly remember the teacher telling me in front of the entire class

that I would never pass my 'O' Level examinations. It was terribly humiliating to have fallen from the top to the bottom of the pile! It was a strong wake-up call, to say the least. But I did not panic. I confronted the tough situation by disbanding my bands and picking up the pieces. I studied extremely hard and the rest is history.

> THE IDEA: Tough situations do not last, but tough people do.

What were your earliest career considerations?

When I was in primary school, my ambition was to be a doctor. To me, it was one of the noblest professions, one that sought the well-being of fellow human beings. I worked towards that but unfortunately, my inadequate 'A' Level results did not allow me admission into the medical faculty of the then University of Singapore.

Resigned that I could not be a doctor, I began exploring other options and opted to do a postgraduate course in fisheries. Halfway through, I left because it was not my calling.

What were early careers like? How have they evolved?

I decided to start working after dropping out of my postgraduate study and aimed to work for a foreign-owned company, as I felt that there were more learning experiences and opportunities to go overseas. As a start, I spent seven years at Mansfield Shipping, where I was involved in dry and bulk liquid shipping, livestock shipping and passenger shipping. I was also given the opportunity to head Mansfield Travel and was appointed the International Marketing Manager for Ben and Company, both of which were associated companies of Mansfield Shipping. I was fortunate because I had the varied experiences that I wanted, from shipping to travel, and to the food business.

But deep in my heart, I always wanted to work for a Singapore-owned company. On my first day at Mansfield Shipping in 1970, I noticed that every office room was occupied by a Westerner, while the Asian executives were sitting outside in the open office. That left an impression on me as a young executive, but I recognised that it was because not many Singaporean executives were ready to take on managerial roles then. We needed time and help to build up those competencies.

After Mansfield, I joined Neptune Orient Lines (NOL), an up-and-coming Singapore company and our national shipping line, where I was offered the opportunity to be based in San Francisco as the head of North America. I always wanted to try an overseas stint because the new environment would broaden my horizons.

After another seven years, I left NOL to join Asia Pacific Breweries Limited (APB) as the General Manager for Singapore. I decided to leave NOL then because I found myself travelling a lot. It hit me particularly hard that I hardly spent time with my two sons who were in primary school then. I told myself that I would stay for seven years in APB, but it grew to be 23 years when I retired at 62. After that, I went on to Frasers and Neave Limited to help out for three years, and I had a three-year contract with them until I was 65. I am now 67, and I am actually still not fully retired.

What are some of your guiding principles?

I learn to seek harmony within myself and with others. Someone wisely said that "harmony of sound is music and the harmony of colour is art". I would add that harmony with oneself and others is good for the soul. This harmonious centre enables me to give my best, combining my many corporate responsibilities with my contributions to society. With regard to the latter, I am most happy to have taken on the chairmanship of the Singapore Kindness Movement and the National Kidney Foundation. The Singapore

Kindness Movement seeks to foster a kinder and more gracious society and the National Kidney Foundation undertakes on-the-ground work with end-stage kidney patients. I visit the dialysis centres on a regular basis and it has been a thoroughly humbling and fulfilling experience for me.

Some people ask me: "Why do you bother to spend so much time with the Singapore Kindness Movement and the National Kidney Foundation? You do not get paid for doing this." My answer is simple. The sick cannot help the sick, and the poor cannot help the poor. We, who are blessed with much, have a duty to take care of those who are suffering around us. It is more blessed to give than to receive.

> THE IDEA: **Great leaders do good and in turn inspire their people towards ethics, integrity and kindness.**

What other principles distinguish you as a leader?

As leaders, we must strive for clarity of thought in both our corporate and personal lives. I achieve this by waking up very early and being at the office by 6am. In the quiet recess of the morning when your mind, heart and spirit are still, that is when ideas begin to flow. Cultivating clarity of thought is very important and I learnt it from Mr David Marshall, our first Chief Minister. When I was a junior executive, I had the privilege of sitting next to him during a dinner and I took the opportunity to ask him what made him such a successful criminal lawyer. He shared his early morning routine of having quiet time to reflect on the things to be done for the day, and the outcomes he hoped to see. I have adopted this practice. When I come into the office in the morning, I feel very fresh and calm, and I reflect on what I want for the company. Not just for the company, but for myself as well. Many business people invest a lot of time thinking about and planning three-, five-, or even ten-year plans for their companies, but we should all have the same depth of thought and planning for our personal lives as well.

Working hard and having good ethics are key factors for professional work. But what distinguishes a competent individual from a successful leader is this ability to have depth in thought. Reflective thinking is not easy – we confront ourselves and our challenges, but it is in these moments that we also develop clear-headed solutions. And it is very much like exercising – the more you do it, the easier it becomes. I derive satisfaction from working with people who have the ability to present a complex problem, verbally or in writing, in a simple and clear manner, as this shows their ability to think reflectively and clearly.

Another principle I believe leaders should possess is a sense of urgency. I never lose sleep if big investments fail, as such investment decisions would usually have been made after a lengthy and deliberate process of planning and analysis. But I do get upset over small things, such as forgetting to do something or procrastinating. These usually result in self-inflicted, unplanned and unnecessary crises. In fact, a lot of crises are needless.

> THE IDEA: **Reflective thinking distinguishes the purposeful leader from the busy one.**

Were you ever confronted with a tough situation in your career?

One of the most challenging situations I faced was when APB was about to invest US$42 million to build a brewery in Ho Chi Minh City about 25 years ago. Vietnam was then in the throes of political and economic reforms. One of my board directors gave me a really hard time, and even remarked that I was crazy to propose investing so much money in such an uncertain and risky environment! I was adamant and insisted that we had to move into Vietnam quickly. I argued that we had done our sums and the company would still be fine even if we were to lose the entire sum of money. I also had to show that it that had to be done for the sake of APB's growth – the market in Singapore was just too small to rely on for profit. The director finally gave his approval as he saw that it was a calculated risk and not a reckless one. Today, the company has five breweries in Vietnam and they are one of the biggest generator of cash flow and profits for the group!

> THE IDEA: Regarding strategic investments, think long-term and be prepared to bear short-term gestation losses, and do not panic or flinch when the situation gets tough.

LEADING OTHERS

How do you build unity among your teams?

I believe that the most effective way is for leaders to invest themselves in the team. I am always with my team in happy times and in sad times, in their professional or personal lives. If they make an honest mistake, I tell them not to have any sleepless nights as I will always support them. Giving them authority and support enables them to feel confident and empowered. That is why APB had the courage to invest in countries such as Cambodia, Myanmar, Laos and Vietnam when no one dared to do so because my team knew that I would support them fully even if they failed. More often than not, such an approach brings out the best in people.

> THE IDEA: Empower your people to take
> calculated risks and back them up when they
> make honest mistakes.

How do you pick the right leaders in your team?

My personal emphasis in terms of leadership development and selection is based on values – sincerity, the ability to learn, humility and whether one is a team player and a people's person. Ultimately, a successful person's main attribute is most likely his or her relational skill. This relational skill can only be built on the foundation of sincerity, honesty and humility, and identifies one as a team player who can influence others to pursue a common goal.

I also recall the late Mr Lee Kuan Yew saying that you can only tell a person's character when he goes through a fire. That is very true – you cannot really tell a person's character until he goes through a crisis and his true values are revealed.

One other invaluable quality I want to mention is equanimity of temperament. I admire people who are not easily agitated and who are always in control regardless of the situation. Only with such a temperament can one achieve greater things, and respond to situations without overreacting.

> THE IDEA: The mark of an outstanding leader is
> his or her relational skills and the test of their
> mantle is through a baptism of fire.

What was your most effective leadership development experience?

I was very blessed to have had many mentors in my corporate career whom I could look up to and learn from. They helped me to reach my potential, often even before I could see it myself. They encouraged and inspired me to attempt great things. They pointed out the pitfalls they encountered before, so that I could avoid the same. Finding a faithful mentor is the most invaluable thing you can do for your own development, in your career or personal lives – they will give you a head start, they will be your cheerleader through your ups and downs and they will cheer you on when you succeed. All that is needed on your part is humility, a willingness to learn and a willingness to ask questions.

Because my mentors set a good example for me to follow, I am humbled that I have the privilege of mentoring others today. Having experienced the deep and personal investment in me by those who walked the corporate walk before me, I feel it is only right that I do the same today.

THE IDEA: **Find a mentor and learn from them.**

LEADING THE ORGANISATION

What were the highlights of your leadership experience with Asia Pacific Breweries?

I look back in quiet and humble satisfaction that my team and I have managed to build a regional giant with APB. When I joined the company, APB (then known as Malayan Breweries Limited) had only five breweries in three countries – two in Singapore, two in Papua New Guinea and one in Malaysia. When I stepped down as CEO, we had a footprint of some 38 breweries across the Asia Pacific. APB currently only lacks presence in Korea, Taiwan, Philippines and Australia. In addition, back in 1986, the market capitalisation of the company was in the region of some S$627 million. In 2013, with the buyout from Heineken, APB's market capitalisation was worth some SG$13.6 billion. I attribute the success of APB to my team who stuck with me through thick and thin, and an extremely supportive Board that believed in us.

On a more personal note, I have spent 42 years in active corporate life, and it has been a very long but satisfying corporate marathon. When I started my corporate life, I always focused on finishing well – to cross the finishing line without stumbling, collapsing or being disqualified. This means completing the race with integrity and contributing positively to the community. To have made it through relatively unscathed and even being able to look back with some fondness is certainly a highlight and achievement I take some professional pride in.

KWEK KOK KWONG
Chief Executive Officer
NTUC Learning Hub

CLARITY IN PURPOSE
AND COMMUNICATION

KWEK KOK KWONG is the Chief Executive Officer of NTUC LearningHub (LHUB®) and is concurrently the Deputy CEO at NTUC First Campus. After serving with distinction in the Singapore Armed Forces (SAF) for 27 years and retiring as a Brigadier General, Kok Kwong decided to join the National Trades Union Congress (NTUC) to promote lifelong learning and education.

In his career in the SAF, Kok Kwong held various key organisational appointments, in areas such as air force operations, organisational transformation, defence policies and relations as well as intelligence. He also held directorship appointments on the Boards of ST Aerospace Engines Pte Ltd and ST Electronics (Info-Comm Systems) Pte Ltd.

Kok Kwong graduated with a Bachelor of Arts majoring in Mathematics from the University of Cambridge in 1989 and a Master of Art from the same university in 1993. In 2001, under a SAF scholarship, Kok Kwong graduated with a Master in Public Administration in 2002 from Harvard University and was awarded the Lucius N. Littauer Fellow award for his outstanding performance.

Kok Kwong is an avid sportsman. He loves trail running and marathons. He is also a keen golfer.

LEADING YOURSELF

What are some of your leadership and/or career transitions? How did you end up being the CEO of NTUC Learning Hub?

When I was a young boy, I always admired charismatic leaders, those who were able to attract people to follow them. Many of them did not have formal education in leadership, and yet they were still able to lead effectively. That intrigued me, so along the way I mirrored and picked up some of these leadership skills from them, and refined them into my own formula. I applied this when I was in the hockey and cross-country teams in junior college, and as a prefect and student counsellor.

The first time I had formal education on leadership was when I was enlisted into National Service and was selected to go to Officer Cadet School in 1986. There, I learnt a lot more about leaders, theories of leadership, how to motivate others, how to form a winning team and how to lead in difficult situations. My 20-plus years with the SAF have given me many golden opportunities to learn, reflect and put into practice what I learnt in the books. I was also given opportunities to lead people from very diverse backgrounds: full-time national servicemen, recruits, people from different age groups, social backgrounds, educational background, etc.

After I left the SAF, I was fortunate to be given the opportunity to lead the NTUC LearningHub, a social enterprise responsible for transforming people's lives through continuous education and training. Training is an area that I am passionate about and can contribute in.

Do you have a role models who has inspired you to become the leader you are now?

One of them is Jack Welch, who led General Electric through tough times and eventually built a sustainable culture in the organisation that stood the test of time. I really like his "4E1P" framework that he used for hiring people:

- Energy
- Energising
- Edge
- Execute
- Passion

"Energy" refers to the drive that pushes the individual to strive for excellence. The individual should also able to energise those around him. "Edge" refers to the special ability to make good decisions when the opportunity arises. The person must then be able to execute his plans in order to achieve results. More importantly, the person must have passion for the job; Welch describes it as a "deep authentic excitement" for the work. While money is a factor, what really drives a person is passion, which provides the fuel that drives a person to do something without feeling tired easily.

THE IDEA: Develop a "4E1P" disposition within yourself and look out for talent who exhibit similar traits and your organisation will go a long way.

How have you applied your leadership model, be it with the Air Force or with NTUC LearningHub?

The "4E1P" framework was one of the models I implemented in the course of my work. But along the way, I came up with my own principles and formulas. I feel that clear communication is crucial in leadership. Without it, your team would not be able to understand what is on your mind, the rationale behind doing certain things and what the company stands for. Therefore, if you want to be an effective leader, spend at least a third of your time thinking of how to communicate effectively.

In order to communicate effectively, one must be able to *think* effectively and clearly. If you do not have clarity in your mind, your communication will naturally be garbled. A leader must therefore have clarity in goals, clarity in strategy, clarity in plans and so on. Once you have these basic clarities in mind, think of how to communicate them effectively. I have come across great plans and strategies many times, but communication would often break down because they were not distilled into a form that could be easily understood and assimilated.

THE IDEA: The clarity of your communication is a clear reflection of the clarity of your thought. Many leaders spend a lot of their time thinking and even more time thinking about how to communicate their thoughts effectively.

What gets you out of bed everyday?

There is a saying that "the purpose of life is to lead a life of purpose". Life is short and we must make the best of it. If you lead a life of purpose, you will discover that you have a greater reservoir of energy than others who do not. Our purpose at NTUC LearningHub is to deliver the social mission of helping people to gain work and life skills that can transform and better their lives, helping them to remain employable, and to grow and improve themselves through lifelong learning.

For me, what gets me out of bed is the sense of fulfilment from making a difference to people. At LearningHub, we train 200,000 trainees yearly, which translates to 600 touch points every day. Through these courses, I hope to be able to make a difference to their lives with a multiplier effect. For instance, I hope that the training will enable them to accomplish their job more easily or find an increase in their employability. In turn, this may give them a better means of supporting their family. When someone comes to me to say, "thank you, you have transformed my life", it really makes my day.

> THE IDEA: Having a great sense of purpose in life will provide you with the fuel to power your life to greater heights.

Prioritisation and time management is always a challenge for leaders. What are some of the best practices that you have with regard to managing your time?

To me, effective time management involves a few things. First, it is about planning to do and doing as planned. I believe that a lot of us do have a vision, but often do not sit down to draw up an action plan. Without one, there is no way the vision will become a reality. After mapping it out, we also need the discipline to carry out our plans.

Second, time is a limited resource. As such, we have to prioritise the things that are important to us. At the start of the week, I prioritise the things that are most important to me. Next, I will plan how to deliver the items that are high on my list. As an example, health is important to me and I commit myself to running on a regular basis. In fact, I run three marathons a year and about 40 to 50km weekly. You don't have to run as much to stay fit. If health is important to you, do something about it and devote some time to it. It isn't too difficult to dedicate half an hour a day to running. Just watch less TV, for example. One must be able to manage time and not let it control you. Most of us are guilty of the latter.

Finally, for items that I am unable to pack into my busy schedule, I multitask. Think creatively and you will find a solution. For instance, I aim to read a book every fortnight but this is not an easy thing to achieve given my schedule. So, I resolved this by obtaining audio books and playing them while I was driving or running. I listened to one or two chapters a day while driving and bingo, I achieved my goal.

Time management is really about having the discipline to have an action plan, executing your action plan and finding creative ways to fit in the things you would otherwise have not been able to.

> THE IDEA: **Time is always a scarce resource for leaders. Planning, prioritisation and creative multitasking will help you to fulfil your key priorities for the week.**

We define leaders by their successes, but they do fail sometimes. What are your thoughts and experiences about not meeting a benchmark and how do you climb back from failure?

In my mid-thirties, I felt like I had plateaued. So I took a course on neurolinguistic programming (and eventually became a certified NLP practitioner). In the process, I learnt to take criticism as a form of constructive feedback and that there was no such thing as failure, only feedback that I could respond to and then move on. I learnt how to reset myself quickly so that I could move on and not be set back by mistakes in life. As leaders, we must be the first to bounce back and set an example for our followers to recover from mistakes and move on quickly, and most importantly, turn adversity into opportunity.

> THE IDEA: The ability to reset oneself, bounce back from setbacks and move on is what I call the personal mastery of resilience and it is a key attribute required of any leader.

Using the words from the title of Rob Goffee's and Gareth Jone's book, "why should anyone be led by you"?

I regard myself as a visionary who can sense the future and look out for potential roadblocks or opportunities. There are three types of people:

- The ones who miss opportunities even if they are right before your eyes.
- The ones who, when given the opportunity, would exploit it.
- The ones who hunt around for opportunities.

A leader should ideally always be looking for new ways to grow the organisation. Followers always like to be with those who hunt for opportunities and I like to think that I belong to that category.

LEADING OTHERS

What are your thoughts or guidelines when you lead others?

A leader must be a good communicator, be it through email, face-to-face or when running a meeting. This is because clarity gives people security. When there is no clarity, people might feel frustrated and lost.

The second part of communicating is about engaging them. It is important to explain the motivations behind doing something. When people are motivated and understand why something is done, you will not need to micromanage them. Many of us spend more time on *what* to do without spending enough time on *why* we are doing it. As the organisation gets bigger, you need to spend more time telling them why something is being done. When the people at the next level are able to understand the why, they will be able to figure out what to do.

I also think that "360-degree communication" is also important. I often tell people to think of issues two levels up and two levels down. For example, I need to understand what are the strategic imperatives of my boss and where possible, the imperatives of his boss as well. I also try to understand what is happening two levels below, as well as what is happening around me. This communication is important because a leader does not operate alone. He operates within an ecosystem that comprises people above, below and around him, whether they are colleagues, superiors, contemporaries or stakeholders.

> THE IDEA: When people are motivated and
> understand the "why" of doing something, they do
> not need to be micromanaged. Always think two
> levels above and two levels below so that you have
> a holistic 360-degree view of issues facing the
> organisation.

Are leadership skills gained by nature or nurture, and can they be trained?

As the CEO of LearningHub, I would like to believe that anything can be taught. Admittedly, leadership is difficult to codify, unlike manufacturing or engineering, for example, where there are concrete steps to follow. Leadership is a mixture of art and science. I would say that art is nature while science is nurture. If one is not a born leader, he should not be disheartened because there is still the "science" to leadership. There are many books on leadership, such as John Maxwell's *Leadership Rules*, which breaks down leadership into 21 rules. I believe that leadership can be learnt and applied to individual circumstances.

That said, I think that people like to follow someone who is sincere and authentic and not one who is just following the principles of leadership with no sincerity. So while you may not be the most charismatic leader, so long as you are sincere and authentic, you will have followers naturally.

> THE IDEA: You can read all the leadership books
> in the world and be well versed in all its rules and
> principles, but without sincerity and authenticity,
> you will not earn the trust of your followers.

In your perspective, what is the unique challenge for Asian leaders and what do you think they should do in order to have a greater presence on the global stage?

This is my personal observation and I do not want to generalise. I feel that we can do better in terms of communicating more effectively and this is something that I am working towards. Another area is innovation. There are many great ideas that have evolved from the west, but there an increasing number of good ideas emerging from the east too. I am hopeful that Asian leaders will narrow the gap in due course.

> THE IDEA: To survive in a dynamic world, strive to be innovative and communicate effectively across the globe beyond culture and boundaries.

LEADING THE ORGANISATION

You mentioned leadership challenges that you had to go through and you also wrote about some challenges when you first joined the company. Would you like to elaborate on them?

When I first joined the company, it was going through a growth spurt. We had a lot of new projects; some were progressing well and some were not. It was a challenging time and we had to grapple with all the projects simultaneously, so there was a high level of stress within the organisation. The first thing I focused on was to quickly build rapport with my colleagues since I was new to the organisation. I stayed open-minded and did not jump to conclusions. A mentor once told me that I should not rush to change anything in an organisation within the first three months.

Many organisations already have gone through sweat and tears and accumulated great corporate wisdom in the process. Instead, an incoming leader should talk to people and appreciate their input and then determine what positive things to keep before thinking about what to change.

> THE IDEA: As a new leader, resist the temptation to change anything until the first three months have passed, when you understand the workings of the organisation and have spoken with the people. First keep the positive things in the organisation and then decide what to change.

What are the top few challenges LearningHub is experiencing in light of the changes within the industry?

The first challenge is that of talent retention. In the current tight labour market, retention is always challenging. As employers, we must engage our staff, groom them and give them opportunities to progress to the next level. Create a cordial working environment so that it is a pleasant place to work at.

The second point relates to the dynamic economic environment. Always scan the horizon to find out what the new training demands are. For instance, as the population becomes more IT savvy, we must embrace e-learning as the technology is mature and the new generation is ready to embrace it.

What is your vision for NTUC LearningHub and how are you going to make it happen?

While it is nice to be comfortable, I always advise others to spend 20% of their resources thinking of the future. At LearningHub, we have a department dedicated to developing future solutions. Their job is to think of new projects and new industries to support in terms of learning. Our vision is to strengthen the company by at least 10% to 15% every year, and to reach even more people in the workforce. Our job is to reach and serve 80% of the workforce, so understanding their requirements is important to us.

> THE IDEA: Dedicate 20% of your time and resources to plan for the future and innovate new ways of doing things.

What do you think are some of the key skills that workers in Singapore will need to have in the next five years?

As Singapore is a service and financial hub, service excellence skills are crucial. In the past, the Singapore economy revolved around manufacturing and our survival relied on how fast and cheaply we were able to produce things. Subsequently, the focus was on who could package things better. However, the new economy is about experience – the company who can deliver the best experience to the client or customer will win the competition. In order to deliver this experience, I think we need to imbue a stronger service mindset by pre empting and delivering the needs of the customer, whether you are in the hospitality, retail or banking industry.

We also need to imbue Professionals, Managers, Executives and Technicians (PMETs) with soft skills encapsulated by a framework. I call this the L.I.F.E. Plus framework, which consists of four groups of skills:

- Leadership
- IT/Innovation
- Finance
- Entrepreneurship

PMETs should first have leadership skills, which we have discussed. Secondly, they should be creative and must constantly strive to innovate by leveraging on IT for productivity. Thirdly, it is important to have at least a basic understanding of finance. Lastly, they should also have an entrepreneurial spirit to think of ways to grow the organisation, be it in terms of finding opportunities, building new ideas, marketing, branding or sales. People equipped with this set of skills would be able to navigate many jobs. Finally, for any individual to progress, one must have self-awareness of his or her limitations and strengths in order to know how to upgrade oneself and move up the career ladder.

> THE IDEA: Continue to upgrade yourself using the L.I.F.E Plus framework and you will grow from strength to strength.

What is your advice to people who aspire to be leaders in your organisation?

Being a leader always seems glamorous, but in order to be one you must be prepared for hard work. Behind the glamour there is always a lot of thinking involved. Before I communicate with my staff, I spend time thinking about the strategy and how to communicate simply and effectively. A leader also needs to spend time engaging his or her staff and understanding and solving their issues. So if you are prepared for hard work and heavy responsibility, go for it!

MATTHEW LANG
Corporate Vice President and
Head of Southeast Asia & Oceania CU
Sony Mobile Communications

BRINGING OUT THE BEST
IN YOUR TEAM

As Corporate Vice President and Head of Southeast Asia &
Oceania CU, MATTHEW LANG is responsible for the Sony
Mobile business in countries across Southeast Asia and Oceania
(excluding Japan, China and Hong Kong).

Matthew joined Sony Mobile after a long and illustrious
career with Sony Corporation, bringing a depth of experience
in sales and marketing roles around the world. In the last 20
years, he has lived and worked in Western Europe, Eastern
Europe, Central Asia, the Caucasus and Africa.

Prior to this appointment, Matthew was the Managing
Director of the Sony South Africa Market Unit for four years.
Initially responsible for achieving a 50 per cent growth in sales

and establishing a clear lead in the LCD TV market for Sony, he went on to lead the successful hosting of Sony's FIFA World Cup sponsorship.

From 2005 to 2007, Matthew was the Managing Director of Sony Nordic and oversaw sales and marketing operations in seven countries. Under his leadership, having restructured the organisation, the team achieved a return to profitability within two years while growing market share. He also held various management roles throughout his career in Sony, including Vice President of e-Commerce and CRM for Europe and Managing Director of Turkey.

Matthew holds a Certified Diploma in Accounting and Finance and a Masters degree in Production Engineering from the University of Cambridge. He is fluent in English, French and German and is married with two children.

LEADING YOURSELF

How did you progress in your career to become the ASEAN CEO of Sony Mobile?

I started by getting an education in engineering at Cambridge. It was not a place I expected to go to – I thought it was too posh and high level for me. Cambridge prides itself not so much in the way it teaches its students, but in the way that the individual colleges supervise the students. They have a supervision system that is either one-on-one or one-on-two with the professor, which instilled in me a big sense of curiosity and a questioning of everything. What they taught me was not just to learn the answer to a question, but to probe the question itself, to think and come up with the answers rather than just learning by rote.

That was in the 1980s and after my education, I went into management consulting. I worked as a consultant for four to five years and was based in London. That gave me great opportunities to experience a diverse range of industries, from insurance and banking to manufacturing and retail. After that, it was time to get a proper job. I applied for Sony and I've been with Sony ever since.

What made you stay in Sony all these years?

I guess the reason I've been with Sony for so long is because they sent me on a wonderful journey around the world and I've been given many opportunities to work in different areas of the business. I started off in corporate planning and strategy, and I did some finance work. I moved into administrations and operations, then marketing and sales, and general management. The great thing about a global company is that it gives you the opportunity to move around the world and that appeals to my natural curiosity and openness to new cultures. I've been successful with Sony, and the last piece of the jigsaw puzzle was being sent to South Africa to run the business when the last Football World Cup was being held in South Africa. There was a need for somebody like me to take charge of the business and make sure that everything went according to plan. While I was there, I bumped into the CEO of Sony Ericsson at the time. He asked me to join Sony Mobile and my answer throughout my career has always been yes. If there is a fork in the road and there is an opportunity to do something different and exciting, I will always say yes. You just have to be open to the things happening around you. I came to Singapore three years ago, and I've been running the mobile business since then.

THE IDEA: Say yes to new challenges and learning
opportunities. You never know where they will
take you.

Who are some of your role models and what have you learnt from them?

About 10 to 15 years ago, I was fortunate to work with a boss
called Derry Newman who, like me, was also quite young. We were
given responsibility for e-solutions, the customer relationship
management (CRM) activities and e-commerce activities for Sony
in Europe. We inherited a failing organisation that needed drastic
turnaround and restructuring. Together with Derry and another
finance guy, Simon, we set about restructuring and reforming the
business. That was a very influential experience and I learnt a lot
from Derry in the process. He wasn't prescriptive and encouraged
me and the rest of the team to rely on our strengths to build
up a team and look at things in the way that I'd been taught in
Cambridge – look at the situation, analyse the situation and come
up with a solution. The great thing was that it was a new business,
so there were no real models that we were forced to follow and it
was mainly up to us.

Being English and being very passionate about rugby, I was very
impressed by Clive Woodward, the coach of the England rugby team
who won the Rugby World Cup in 1994. He went from business
to sport, and combined business leadership techniques with sport
psychology. He was very detailed, he made sure that no stone was
left unturned and that all the details were looked after. Rugby is
a sport that has evolved from being an amateur sport played by
people who were just passionate about the game to one that is now
very professional. I think the England team in the mid 1990s had
a lot to do with that, where they brought in a lot of management

techniques and analysis into the game, and subsequently became the best in the world. That was very inspirational for me. It's not an individual who wins a football match or rugby match, it's the team that wins and it's the same in business – it's about building a team. No man is bigger than the team, and the team is greater than sum of all of its parts if it is a real high-performance team. I think there is a lot of inspiration and learning I could take from that.

The last role model is Nelson Mandela. I was fortunate enough to be in his home country for four years. He's someone who really knows what his core values are, sticks to them and sees things through.

> THE IDEA: No man is bigger than the team and certainly not his/her ego!

With those role models, what kind of principles do you live by?

For me, it's about integrity and honesty, openness to new ideas, communication and being decisive.

What do you think makes a good leader?

I understand my values and stick to them. I am very clear about what it is I want to achieve, how I want to achieve it and how I want to behave. In terms of leadership, I build high-performance teams. I'm not afraid of bringing people who are far superior to me in terms of ability and potential into the team. I always see my job as bringing out the best possible performance for the people in my team. Before that, it's about getting the best possible players into that team. I can then lead that team with decisiveness and clarity of vision, and I will empower the team to perform to the best of its abilities. It is not so much about me succeeding, but about the team achieving its goals.

I think one of the tests of being a good leader is whether people are willing to follow you and move on with you if you have changed companies.

> THE IDEA: To build a high-performing team, you have to be comfortable enough to recruit the best possible players even when they may be better than you.

What are some techniques that leaders use to manage their time and energy?

What is most important is energy. Time is finite and cannot be changed, while energy is expandable. If we are to perform at the best of our abilities, we need to optimise our energy rather than our time. Time will take care of itself if you manage your energy.

I put in place a culture that is much more about energy management than time management. I want people to perform to the best of their abilities on tasks that will add long-term value. While acknowledging that there are urgent things that need to be done, if we really want to have a team that performs at its peak, the long-term added-value jobs need to be prioritised and done when people have maximum energy. By energy, I mean physical energy, emotional energy, mental energy and spiritual energy. They need to be fit and not tired, they need to be aware of their emotions in terms of how they impact others and on their own performance. They need to be able to focus and to prioritise between what adds long-term value and what is just urgent. Everything needs to be aligned with their spiritual or core values so that they are not doing a job they absolutely hate or do not believe in.

> THE IDEA: Leaders often underestimate the impact of their emotions on the team. Be cautious that you do not display too much negative emotion at work as team members will pick up on those cues.

What are some practical ways in which you manage your team's energy?

I think the office itself is a good example of that. I encourage people to maintain a healthy lifestyle and to optimise their time. I don't need the staff to be at the office 10 minutes before 9am when everyone in Singapore is trying to get to the office. They come into the office at a time that is convenient, be it 7am to 8am or around 9.30am. I am happy for the staff to start their day working on emails at home and then coming to the office when it only takes them 10 minutes as opposed to 30–45 minutes.

We run leadership courses throughout the year for everybody. We go through energy management principles and try to get people to understand the difference between what is urgent and what adds long-term value. We also try to cut down on the inefficiencies and distractions that modern technology imposes on all of us. I try to show people that if we want to perform at our best, we have to focus on one thing at a time. I think this is a disease of today's environment – people are being distracted all the time and nobody gives full attention to what they need to prioritise. I try to build an office environment based around these principles.

> THE IDEA: Respecting the varied life stages that your employees are going through (and hence the work-life flexibility required) goes a long way in building team engagement and retention.

Share an experience where things did not turn out the way you expected them to, and what you learnt from the experience as a leader.

The way I deal with these trips and falls in the most positive manner is through reflection and trying to look at things through a different lens.

When I was in South Africa, the local organisation that I was with merged with the Middle-East operation. I then had to report to a Japanese boss who was based in Dubai. He had a very different view of how our business should work. It was a view that was primarily founded upon the type of business environment that existed in Dubai. In Dubai, the company was mainly working with distributors, whereas in South Africa, we were very retail-focused and worked with small local retailers and some big retailers throughout South Africa. Our two worldviews conflicted massively. As he was the boss, I had to temper my view of how the business should be run. In the end, I found a solution by delivering what I needed to deliver for the FIFA World Cup and then thankfully finding a way out into another part of the business through the Sony Mobile connection.

Looking back on this, it was a very stressful time for me. The business did not work very well because we had conflicting views about how the business should be managed and decisions that I did not agree with were made. I can see and understand why the person with whom I was fighting had a different view. It's easier to reflect and put yourself in someone else's shoes when you have a way out of that, but that was how I exited with a fair degree of positivity.

THE IDEA: Having two co-heads or sharing decision-making responsibilities with another manager can create conflicts. To make the best of the situation, each co-head should aim to see the other's perspective and communicate often with each other to ensure trust and communicate unity to the team.

LEADING OTHERS

What principles do you subscribe to when leading your team at Sony?

The most important is communication as a leader. We can never communicate enough, be it communicating with the team here, with my peers in the rest of the world or with my managers above me. Communicate both ways, communicate a strategy so that the team here understands it, communicate the challenges and the support that we need up and throughout the organisation – it's a cliché, but there can never be too much communication.

Be decisive, don't hesitate when making a decision. Make the decision and then communicate. If the decision is wrong, communicate and change that.

Always look to perform to the best of your abilities. We are always looking at the performance of the team, how we can improve and what we need to improve as a team.

THE IDEA: It is better to make a wrong decision and change it for the better than to sit on a decision and do nothing.

How do you attract and retain talent to build an effective team?

I am not shaken when someone leaves because it is a fantastic opportunity to bring some new talent into the business. No matter how critical or important the person who leaves is, it opens up an opportunity. I love the opportunity that recruiting gives. I use a lot of instinct to gauge personality fit. I leave the technical, functional stuff to the HR team, but I am looking for someone with the personality and culture that can fit into and work with the team.

I am unafraid to hire people that are better than me. In that respect, I try to be as humble as I possibly can. It is not me that runs the business; it's the guys that I bring into the team who are going to make the business succeed. I want only the best.

> THE IDEA: While we do our best to retain key talent in the team, departures can also present a great opportunity to recruit new ideas and fresh energy.

What are some questions that you ask to find that sort of talent?

I look at what drives a person, what their aspirations are, where they see themselves in the future. I also look at their strengths and ask for examples of what they have done in their careers where they really felt that they were performing at their best. What did it feel like when you hit the zone? What were you doing?

Was there a leadership challenge that you had to handle with regard to your team? What did you gain from that experience?

I was put in charge of a Nordic company based in Denmark. It was a failing business that needed turning around, and I had just come from my experience in e-commerce and CRM. I was very passionate about the need for change and the benefits that dramatic change can bring to the business.

I went into the business and was very decisive. I chopped two or three of the senior leadership team almost immediately. We had to make some retrenchments. I came in a bit like a bull in the china shop, wielding a sword. We resized the business, set a new direction and vision, and brought some new talent into the team. We were reasonably successful in turning that business around, but what I learnt over the next two to three years was that I really scared everybody. I did exactly what the Sony leadership had requested and what was needed, but I learnt about the impact that a leader can have on the team and how important and influential that is. Even though I had done all the right things, the emotional impact was deep-seated. As I was exiting the business after two and a half years, people came to tell me that they were petrified. It was a very good lesson. Even though you are doing the right thing, the way you do it and the impact it has on the organisation are very important.

If I were to do it again, I would do it differently. I would communicate more about why I was doing it and get a team that communicated throughout the organisation more clearly and openly. I was much younger then and thought I was doing the right thing, without thinking about the impact it would have on the 150 people in the organisation in four to five different countries. We needed a stronger and broader communication platform to work with everybody and to give them time to understand what we were doing. There should also have been more discussion forums to let people share their emotions and thoughts.

THE IDEA: While tough decisions need to be made, the style of communication and appreciation of the stakeholders involved can be handled with a softer touch.

LEADING THE ORGANISATION

What is the business currently like in terms of people and numbers?

We have between 100 to 120 people in Sony Asia Pacific. We do not cover China, Japan and India, but look after the rest of Asia Pacific, and are based in Singapore, Malaysia, Indonesia, Australia and with smaller representations in emerging markets such as Thailand, Philippines, Vietnam, Cambodia and Myanmar.

It's a $1-billion turnover business that involves a high amount of sales per head compared to the traditional electronic business, which is much more resource-heavy. We try to run a light operation and need to be very swift in decision-making. Our business is a rapidly changing business, hugely competitive and very fast moving. We introduce products every six months, but so do our competitors and we cannot afford to sit back and relax.

What qualities must a leader have in terms of leading his organisation in this fast-moving industry?

I think you need to be flexible; you need to be able to replan very quickly. The competitive landscape will change dramatically overnight. For example, we work within Sony Corporation's guidelines to prepare a budget for 12 months and a mid-range plan for three years. But by the time we've prepared our budget, the situation has already changed. In our business, there's a big focus on planning, making sure that we have our forecast volumes in place so that the factories can produce the products that are needed immediately. If we get any of this wrong, the product does not move and we would be completely stuck. It's not a business where you have two to three months' leeway; we really just have today and the next three to four weeks.

We work within the planning assumptions and guidelines that Sony Corporation sets us, but we have our own internal forecasting and planning process that has to be much more flexible. What I love about it is that we have a small team communicating very often and very closely. I love being able to sit down with the teams. We have an operational organisation and the factory staff and product development staff are also flexible and adaptable to changes. It is an energising environment to work in and be part of.

Is there something unique about leading in Asia that is different from other countries or regions that you've managed?

For me, no. It's about the people and the team. The people that I'm working with here are predominantly Asians, and I've had to learn about and adapt to the culture. Although the culture in Singapore is different from American, Swedish or European culture, the fundamentals of leading a team here are no different to leading a team in Africa, Europe, America or anywhere else in the world. The fundamentals of what I try to bring to the team and to my leadership style have worked here just as well as they worked in Europe or Africa.

There are differences and nuances. When I first arrived, I felt that many in the organisation were waiting to be told what to do instead of coming up with proactive suggestions on how we could improve things. There was a deep Asian culture in place. My predecessors had all been Japanese, and the organisation was very used to instructions coming from the big boss. My philosophy is very different – I can tell you what the priorities are and what I want to achieve, but you are employed to make this happen and you know better than I do about Asian countries, so I need you to tell me what support you need to achieve what we want as a team. This is not a concern anymore because people have adapted and opened up, and are much happier at being empowered to do the things that they are much better at doing than I am. I am here to provide the empowerment and support to enable them to succeed.

What are the current challenges that Sony Mobile Asia Pacific is experiencing?

We are fortunate to be in a region of strong growth. In the developing countries such as Malaysia, Indonesia, Thailand and Vietnam, everybody wants to buy a smartphone. I don't think this demand is so much present in America, Europe or even in Japan.

The challenge in the industry is that there are very big economies of scale. At the moment, there is a duopoly between two strong competitors. They have great barriers to competition in that they have substantial resources to promote and market their brands. Our challenge is to get consumers to first be aware that Sony makes great smartphones, and then to put a Sony Xperia onto the list of their potential smartphone purchases. Finally, our challenge is to convince customers that our product is superior to other alternatives and to break through the brand power that our competitors currently enjoy.

The good thing is that things change very quickly in this industry. The big challenge for me in Asia Pacific and for Sony Mobile around the world is to promote our brand to the best of our abilities in the most efficient and effective manner with the resources that we have, and accepting that those resources are far smaller in terms of finance. We have to find innovative and creative ways to promote our products, and more importantly for the industry, it is becoming less about the product and more about what you can do with the product and the ecosystem that surrounds that product. That is where Sony has potential; we have a great stable of media assets, exciting products and content that consumers love.

How are you going to make it happen?
I will move forward with the same values and philosophy – getting the best people into the team and enabling them to perform to the best of their abilities. In doing so, we will bring innovation and creativity into how we communicate with our customers, continue to produce the products that are the best in class and build on the momentum that we've been building for the last couple of years. We believe that things change quickly and there are tipping points in the industry. Once we reach those tipping points, we believe that we have a really strong story that consumers are going to love.

Sony Mobile is an open and collaborative company that matches my own philosophy and culture. We don't want to negatively affect our biggest partners such as operators, distributors and retailers around the world; we don't try to go over the top as others do. We are much more open to working with them to create services and content and enhance user experience. That is how we are going to succeed. We believe we have a clear vision, product technology and content and services that will make us successful. We have come a long way over the last couple of years since we've switched to producing only smartphones.

> THE IDEA: The advantage when you are not the market leader is to be able to customise your service and content to a niche group of users who will be loyal to you because you listened to their needs.

Are there any issues and challenges with your senior management who are typically Japanese? How do you circumvent those problems?

There's definitely a Japanese culture. Japanese management is very consensus-based where they have already reached a consensus prior to any given meeting and the meeting is just a rubber-stamping of what has been agreed. It's also very hierarchical, and there's a lot of respect paid to one's age rather than experience and ability. I've experienced all these in my 25 years with Sony, and despite the differences with Anglo-Saxon norms, I've survived and thrived. I think one of the most important things when working with the Japanese is to build trust. It's an important value and one of my core values as well. Once you can establish trust, the Japanese system will support you.

I guess I've also survived by being different. I am prepared to be controversial, but at the same time, I understand that I am working in a Japanese environment so I can't be too extreme. I've been fortunate to have some good bosses who are prepared to give me space. I must have gained their trust, and once the trust is there, they are willing to gamble with me.

Very early on, I was working in the European headquarters in Germany, and we were expanding to Eastern Europe. The Japanese boss I was working for used to give me a lot of business plans to build using my consulting experience and education. He grew to trust my intellectual and communication capabilities in putting together those business plans. When the time came for me to move back to the UK, he asked me to move to Eastern Europe instead and be the head of marketing, which was a huge promotion. That's an example of trust being established.

> THE IDEA: Regardless of the main nationality
> or culture of your company's management, the
> fundamental step to managing one's bosses is to
> gain their trust.

What was Sony Mobile like before you took over? After three years leading this sector of the business, what are your key achievements?

Primarily, I built a team that is now capable of driving the business. We now have a team that is much more cohesive and that understands the opportunities they have in each market. I've transformed the organisation from a traditional regional headquarters in Singapore that controls and manages market units out in the field, to one that has business being driven in the field and supported by a team of experts in Singapore. This team is there to set directions, but mainly to support and empower the business in the field. I think it's a much more sustainable culture and business.

Over the three years that I've been here, we've moved the business completely from being a feature phone business to a 100% mobile computing smartphone business. That hasn't been my doing, but by the product development team at the corporate level. We now have an organisation in Asia Pacific that is entirely focused on how to develop the smartphone business and the mobile computing business. It is much more empowered and energetic than it was in the past, and much freer of spirit and inspired. With values aligned to the jobs that they are doing, and by putting that kind of culture in place, I hope that I have a more innovative team. I think that by building the right culture and environment and empowering people, you will get innovation.

What would you give as a final word of advice to a young, aspiring Sony talent?

Learn to be open, learn the power of communication. Make sure that you are in a job in a company that matches your values. Make sure that you are clear about what it is that you want to do; don't do something that other people want of you. Do something that is aligned with your values that you can derive satisfaction from. With all of these, you will get to where you want to be.

CAROL FONG
Chief Executive Officer
CIMB Securities

LITTLE GESTURES CREATE
BIG IMPACT

CAROL FONG is the Chief Executive Officer of CIMB Securities (Singapore) Pte Ltd and Head of the Equities Division of CIMB Group, headquartered in Singapore. In her present role, Carol is responsible for the overall management and financial performance of the entire Group's equities business, a regional franchise covering Asia (ex-Japan), as well as major financial centres such as London and New York.

Carol's extensive experience in financial markets spans over 30 years. She started her career at OCBC Bank, where she worked for five years. Over the last 25 years, she has held a number of senior managerial positions in various stockbroking firms. She is also currently Chairman of the SGX Securities Advisory Committee.

LEADING YOURSELF

What are the highlights of your career transitions?

One of my first jobs was in Human Resources (HR) – I was in HR for five years at Oversea-Chinese Banking Corporation (OCBC Bank). I am a strong believer that HR is an important function, and I think that's where I learnt a lot of my EQ skills when working with branch managers. I then switched to doing credit for two years at OCBC before deciding to make a career switch to fund management. I was invited to join a stockbroking company, J.M. Sassoon by a client which initiated my career in the securities world. I spent about three to four years there before I got invited back to OCBC because it was starting up its own securities firm. I spent about five to six years at OCBC before being invited to join Vickers Ballas. Vickers was then bought over by DBS. It was at DBS where I transitioned from a senior sales head role to a bigger management role. I then got invited to join G.K. Goh, which was subsequently bought over by CIMB.

How did you end up becoming the CEO of CIMB?

When I joined G.K. Goh in 2004, we were bought over by CIMB a year later. After the merger, I was made Group Head of Institutional Equities in CIMB-GK and subsequently made CEO in mid-2008. In 2012, we bought the Royal Bank of Scotland (RBS) franchise, which was an even bigger merger because we moved away from ASEAN to go into Asia, which included countries such as Korea, India, Taiwan, Australia and Hong Kong. That took a lot of hard work.

Who are the role models in your career and what lessons have you learnt from them?

My previous group CEO, Dato' Sri Nazir Razak, who is now the chairman of CIMB Bank. He, to me, is a role model. He never used his family connections to move up the corporate ranks and instead worked hard from the ground up and moved all the way through the ranks to become CEO. He's a great visionary and I truly admire him and look to him as a role model in terms of my own career.

Mr G.K. Goh himself is a person that believes a lot in a personal touch – if you're loyal to him, he's loyal in return. He taught me a lot about loyalty and to look after your own people. He's the kind of person that would go out on a limb to personally help someone.

What are some of the principles that you live by as a leader? What would you advocate when you're talking to your teams?

As leaders, it's easy to be at the top and tell everyone to do things. I always believe that at the top level, you also have to walk the talk. If you expect people to do certain things, you have to be able to do it as well. There are some leaders who delegate things and expect to have them done, but I take a different philosophy. You need to know the nuts and bolts of the business, especially in our business, in order to get respected. Leading by example and walking the talk are some of the things I measure myself against when it comes to leadership. The rest is quite normal for any leader – the focus on profitability and the business.

> THE IDEA: You get much more respect from your followers when you are able to "walk the talk" instead of being a boss who merely forwards emails.

What are some examples that you practice every day when you say "lead by example"?

I mean really little things. For example, we expect all our sales and research people to come for morning meetings at 7.30am. I attend the morning meetings as well just to show them that I work equally long hours.

I also make it a point to send everybody in the Singapore team a birthday card. A lot of them are very appreciative of the fact that you remember their birthday and that they get a card from the CEO. Sometimes, monetary rewards are not enough to keep people loyal to you, so it's these little touches that matter.

> THE IDEA: Adding personal touches to your leadership style can do wonders to engage team members – start by writing them a birthday card or a note of appreciation at the end of the year.

What goes on in your mind as a CEO?

At the end of the day, we run a business. You do have to make sure that your businesses are moving in the right direction and that you're bringing in the profits. At the same time, you also have to ensure that you haven't forgotten the employees. It's a balancing act because you want to attract and pay employees, and maintain profitability for the firm.

Sometimes we also have to make hard decisions. If costs are too high, you have to make a cold decision to rationalise and that's not easy because you know that you're impacting not only the employees, but their families as well. These are not easy decisions to make, but as CEO, you have to make such decisions. It's not the most pleasant thing to do, but it has to be done.

Do you have the practice of managing your time on a day-to-day basis?

I've never worked as hard before as I'm working now. I work longer than 12 hours, and effectively, it's around 18 to 19 hours a day.

During the day, people want to see you and talk to you. There are a lot of meetings: board meetings, management meetings, you meet the vendors and you meet the consultants, etc. And the only time you actually have to look at your emails is at night. I make it a point to clear all my emails when I go back home. That's what I learnt from one of my former bosses, when he was Chairman of OCBC Bank. He had a philosophy that if he asks a question, he wants it to be answered within 24 hours. This was instilled into me since day one and I've always tried to respond within 24 hours for everything that comes to me. It's something you have to do; if you don't, it snowballs.

> THE IDEA: Do not be the bottleneck where decisions are pending because you have not addressed them. Have a policy of responding to emails within a certain time frame, even if it is to communicate that you need more time to deliberate on an issue. This instills trust and minimises guesswork from your team.

How do you keep your energy and spirits up?

Enjoy what you're doing. I love my job, but it's not easy. People tend to think that it gets easier the higher you go, but it doesn't. It's a lot harder because at the end of the day, the buck stops with you as the leader. It's like juggling a lot of balls in the air!

> THE IDEA: Being a leader is never an easy job, so you are better off learning to love (all, if not most aspects of) the job!

There's a lot of focus on helping women with unique strengths and challenges to rise in organisations. What's your perspective?

I was quite lucky when I started in the financial industry, the trading hours were very short – effectively you start at 9am and go home at 5pm. I have three kids and I was lucky to start my family in the early stages of my career. I had a lot of help from my parents and parents-in-law, and what I did was to shuttle the kids early in the morning e.g. three days to my mother, three days to my mother-in-law. It's comforting to know that when you are at work, someone in the family is looking after them, in addition to a maid. For any female employee who wants to progress in their career, I think getting parental support is important.

With that comfort, you can concentrate on doing your work, knowing that things are taken care of at home. Because I was in sales, I did not have much administrative work after 5pm. I could spend enough time with my children during their early formative years. With my career now, I spend very little time with them, but the good news is that they are all grown up and have their own lives to lead, although I make sure that we at least have a Sunday lunch together. It's different in their formative years – as a mother, you want to spend more time with your children during those years. That's always a difficult question for most females to answer – do I have a family now, or later? My advice is to have one earlier as I increasingly that find many colleagues who decided to postpone having a family earlier are now having difficulties conceiving.

THE IDEA: Establish stable support systems at home in order for you to focus on your career. Discuss family planning and prioritise having a family with your partner earlier, in line with your career plans.

What advice do you have for women who aspire to be a CEO but sometimes have familial duties and face certain challenges, even within the organisation?

I have noticed that the government is pushing for more gender diversity on Boards, so I'm sure we'll improve even more. Apart from parental support, the employer's support is also very important. As a leader in the organisation, I'm always very supportive when people have to take a day off for their children. It's all part of empowering women.

LEADING OTHERS

When picking your executive team, what do you think makes a great team?

Having the same principles and the same kind of work attitudes help. They have to believe in common objectives and goals. When there are different nationalities there will be cultural differences, it's important to have one culture within the firm. When you have a strong culture in your firm, it sets off related behavioural changes and habits. If you have a wrong culture in place, things can go very wrong.

> THE IDEA: Choose team members for their aptitude, but more importantly, for their consistent attitude and common set of working principles.

How do you bring out the best in your team members?

I think empowering them is very important – you need the ability to delegate and the ability to leave things alone. One of the greatest failings of leaders is that they cannot delegate or cannot find a successor. I've always believed that for you to be successful as a leader, you have to find someone to succeed you, who can do better than you.

For example, I sit on a talent review committee where we put up names and ask who the successor is for every top position and we try to put that in place. This is only a recent phenomenon for CIMB, but I make sure that we identify three to four people before I talk to HR and put them through training and mentorship programmes.

THE IDEA: Success as a leader means that you are not jealously preserving your own seat but able to actively groom successors to take your place. That way you too are ready to take on the next bigger role.

What do you look out for in someone who has leadership potential?

Passion is a key attribute. If you're not passionate about your work, you can't lead your people. If you are not energetic, your people will feel the same way. A leader has to have passion for work and for the organisation, putting the organisation above self. The next thing I look out for is integrity.

You've been headhunted for several jobs. Is inheriting a team challenging? How do you get your team to respect you?

When I came over to G.K. Goh from OCBC, I was appointed as the new head of institutional sales. I was literally a stranger who walked into the room. What I did was to talk to the most senior sales people in the team saying look, this is what I've done, this is what I can do. Are you with me or not? This was within a week of my arrival. They said they were with me, and since they were with me, I would also groom them for the next level. Put your cards on the table and tell the team what you have achieved and what you can do, and ask them if they're with you or not.

> THE IDEA: As the new leader of an established team, it is best to lay your cards on the table and help them to understand why you were appointed as their boss.

What do you do with people who are not with you or say they are with you but don't behave as such?

You'll find out over time, and for those people who don't buy in, you have to manage them out of the team. I've done it a few times. If they are not with you and you try to lead the group in a certain direction, it can be very disruptive for the organisation. I've always believed that you have to nip it in the bud sooner rather than later.

> THE IDEA: A sore wound festers over time and spreads the infection. If you are not able to treat it, it is best to nip it in the bud.

LEADING THE ORGANISATION

What are some unique challenges that arose from these acquisitions and mergers?

Firstly, managing different cultures is challenging. When we took over RBS, we had more than nine different countries coming on board, which meant many different cultures, different ways of doing things, and so on.

The second challenge is how to keep everyone together and mould them into one group. It's been two years since the merger with RBS and we are only seeing things coming together now.

Finally, being empowered by your leader also helps because they have to believe that you are the right person to lead the group.

> THE IDEA: A lot of decisions and changes are at stake when companies are acquired and merged, ranging from culture integration, cost rationalisation and leadership of the combined organisation. It often takes time for the dust to settle before a clear strategy can be put in place.

What's your perspective of a co-head structure?

It works in the short-term, but in the long run, it will not work because things can fall through the cracks – is it your responsibility or mine? No one takes responsibility for that, and at the end of the day, where does the buck stop?

What is your vision for CIMB equities?

If CIMB could become a meaningful player in Asia Pacific, I think I would have achieved the goal set up by the group. We are quite dominant in ASEAN, but we have yet to prove ourselves in markets outside of Asia. It takes time to develop a brand.

How would you develop the CIMB brand?

You need to have a vision and mission statement and prove yourself relevant to your clients. I think the fact that we are one of the few brokers with roots in ASEAN that have expanded into Asia puts us on a very good footing. We brand ourselves as a multi-local player, in the sense that we have many geographies but are also local with a 'feel' of the ground.

What are some of the organisational challenges within the financial industry or in CIMB that you foresee in the next four to five years?

Many say that brokerage is a dying profession; competition is not getting easier with thinner commissions and technological changes. We have to adopt and modify our strategies to meet these challenges.

What are some things that you are investing in to deal with these challenges?

Electronic trading. While some banks such as Nomura have bought external systems such as Instinet and incorporated them within their framework, we are building it up in-house. This may take a longer time, but will allow us to be nimble and customise solutions for our clients.

How would you lead the organisation with all these changes and complexities?

It's not easy in an environment that is increasingly regulated and under scrutiny by the media and public. You need a strong compliance team. You have to strike a balance between complying with the law and at the same time, doing commercial business. Sometimes, as a CEO, you have to make a call. The rule of thumb I always use is: if it's black and white, you definitely have to go with white, but if it's grey, then you make a call. The regulations and interpretations of the law are sometimes unclear, and that's when you may need to make a call.

> THE IDEA: As the leader the buck always stops with you.

What would be your advice for young finance students hoping to be successful in the financial industry?

I always advise my younger peers to think of their careers in five-year buckets. Set yourself a goal for the next five years and if you don't achieve it, recalibrate and decide where you want to go. It has served me well.

> THE IDEA: Think of your career in five-year buckets and set goals and milestones accordingly.

ROD LEAVER
Chief Executive Officer, Asia
Lend Lease

DARING TO DISRUPT

ROD LEAVER joined Lend Lease in January 2008 and was
appointed Chief Executive Officer, Asia in April 2011. Prior to
his current role, Rod was Chief Executive Officer, Australia, and
prior to that, Chief Executive Officer of Asia Pacific and Global
Head of Lend Lease's investment management business, where
he also had responsibility for the UK infrastructure development
business and the US-based public partnership's business.

Rod has extensive experience in the property investment
and funds management industry. He has previously held roles
as Executive Chairman and founder of the listed Ronin Property
Group, managing total funds of A$2.4 billion; co-founded
and worked as Chief Executive Officer of the listed property
investment company, James Fielding Group, where he managed
total funds of A$1.8 billion; and was also a co-founder and

Executive Director of Paladin Australia Limited, managing total funds of A$2.3 billion.

Rod is currently a member of the Singapore government's Urban Redevelopment Authority's Design Advisory Committee. He previously served as a Director of the Green Building Council of Australia and was a member of the Australian government's Business Roundtable on Climate Change. He was also a National Director of the Property Council of Australia and was its New South Wales President for three years. He has also held positions as Chair of the Australian National Business Leader's Forum on Sustainable Development, and sat on the New South Wales government's Heritage Council and their Historic Houses Trust Foundation, as well as the Property Industry Foundation. He is a Fellow of the Australian Property Institute and the Royal Institute of Chartered Surveyors.

LEADING YOURSELF

Could you provide a summary of your career journey and how you ended up being the CEO of Lend Lease Asia Pacific?

Mine is not a typical career path. I grew up in Australia and my father sent me off to boarding school at great expense. He expected me to do well and to go to university. I have always wanted to move forward, but unfortunately find it difficult to focus on certain things sometimes because I am quite creative and can have a short attention span. So I have strengths, but also lots of weaknesses in other areas. I became a very good guitar player in my last year of high school, and failed to graduate. My father was not very happy with that and it was a turning point for me.

> THE IDEA: Don't judge those who make mistakes too harshly but instead encourage them to use it as a learning experience – the biggest failure is to make the same mistake twice.

What was your first job?

I was first employed as a chauffeur by the Chairman of Australia's largest foreign property company but after 12 months in the job, I crashed his Jaguar. But rather than terminate my employment, he very surprisingly and kindly offered me the company's first-ever apprenticeship. At that point, he felt that we got on really well and I was probably the son he never had. I stayed with that company for eight years. The experience was fantastic and they gave me amazing career opportunities to manage various projects. When I was about 22, I was controlling reasonably large developments for them. I then had the opportunity to go to Perth in Western Australia to project manage a major regional shopping centre, and I was only 23 years old at the time.

> THE IDEA: Career opportunities can take place in any form and circumstance. Treat every task, client and boss you have with utmost care as they may just be your next career sponsor.

What did you do after your first career stint?

After that fabulous opportunity, I moved on to couple of other companies and effectively became a jack of all trades as opposed to a master of one. I was not a subject matter expert, but I went to night school at a technical further education college and attained my valuation degree in property. I believe that education is really important, and it was really good advice for me when I was younger. You can't just be all practical; you also have to be theoretical.

A principal founding shareholder of one of the companies I worked for later left and invited me to create a start-up funds management company in 1993. I was 33 at the time. We started that jointly and over the next five years, the business grew to be one of the top 10 property funds management companies in Australia with A$2.4 billion under management. We sold the business to Deutsche Bank in 2000 and created another funds management business that managed circa A$2 billion, which was eventually acquired by Mirvac, an Australian property REIT.

I took nine months off work, and then started my own funds management company. We took over management of a A$2.5 billion REIT owned by AMP in Australia. One of the largest banks in the country invested in my company, and the trust was eventually acquired by Multiplex. Finally, after taking another nine months sabbatical, I was approached to join Lend Lease as Global CEO of Investment Management.

How did you end up at Lend Lease?
Joining Lend Lease was a pretty easy decision because it is a very sustainable company. It's one of the world's leading developers of sustainable buildings and really drives innovation around that. There are many companies around the world I wouldn't want to work for because I think they are largely just focused short-term on the dollars and not on the long-term goal. I believe that sustainable financial returns are really a by-product of getting everything else right. In 2010 I was appointed as CEO of the Australian business.

How did you end up as Asia CEO, Lend Lease?
The opportunity arose, and I put my hand up to run it. This surprised a lot of people as the role was seen to be less "lucrative" than

managing the entire Australian business. But I see it as a disruption for myself. I have a strong belief that you need to disrupt yourself from time to time to shake things up and keep things interesting.

> THE IDEA: **When things start getting too comfortable and routine, leaders have to look for ways to disrupt themselves to reinvent their business or their careers. Avoid disruption to the point of self-destruction though!**

Where Lend Lease is concerned, are leaders better as specialists or generalists?

I am not a subject matter expert but instead a generalist, having had approximately 20 different roles in the property industry – from a research analyst, project manager, asset manager, fund manager, business owner and developer to CEO. Being a jack of all trades is actually quite important as a CEO in Lend Lease because you need to understand and manage an organisation that already has many silos of subject matter expertise such as construction or investment management. In order to run the business, you need to connect the dots across everything to weigh your competitive advantages and make sure that you are extracting the best from everything. If you are just a specialist, you tend not to see the big picture. That's where I believe I have been successful because I have a broad perspective and look for what's right in the long-term as opposed to just the short-term.

What are some of your leadership guiding principles?

I treat everyone just as I would want to be treated, with dignity and respect. Respect is one of Lend Lease's core values, but you have to walk the talk. For me, that translates to humility and I am a great believer in the saying, "rooster one day, feather duster the next". No individual creates anything by themselves. All I can do is lead. As I said earlier, I do have strengths, but I also have some significant weaknesses. Leading involves being self-aware about what those weaknesses are, playing to your strengths and then putting together a strong team of capable people that complement your skills and have diversity of thought. The diversity is critical; we all think we know the answer, but when you have different ways of thinking coming together and the right people with the right skills and the right complementary strengths, you can create amazing outcomes. That, to me, is important.

> THE IDEA: It is better to exemplify your principles
> and values than to preach them. Have the habit
> of walking the floor to actively demonstrate your
> beliefs rather than sending emails to masses.

How do you drive values throughout the organisation and how do they influence behaviour?

We have six values in this company – a number involve trust, respect and collaboration, and the others revolve around innovation. I run the organisation focused on our principles and values, but ultimately they are only words. Behaviours define words, so our behaviour is the most important thing. We have a clear strategy about what we want that drives the organisational structure, and then we put the right people into that structure which, in the long-term, should drive the desired outcome. Ultimately, that will drive the financial performance. That's always difficult in a publicly listed company because there's usually a short-term focus on earnings. Ultimately, we are here for the long-term. I am quite literally the custodian for the next generation of people who come through. I don't have the

right to disrupt this company to the point where it is unsustainable.
I rarely make short-term decisions.

> THE IDEA: A clear organisation strategy drives the
> structure, which attracts talent that fit the roles and
> structures, that in turn drives financial performance.

What drives you as a leader?

Ultimately, what drives me relates to our guiding principles: safety,
sustainability and diversity. My aspiration as a leader is to create
amazing opportunities for the people working in Lend Lease. Winning
work provides career opportunities for everyone in the organisation.
When running your own business, it is just a small business at the
end of the day, whereas Lend Lease is one of the world's greatest
developers and we create amazing urban regeneration projects
around the world.

Who are some of your inspiring leadership role models and what sort of lessons did you learn from them?

My partner in two successful start-up businesses taught me a
couple of important things. One is the ability to view everything as a
learning experience. Even if we experienced a failure, he would never
refer to it as one but instead turn it into something positive. That
was very important to me. It helped me to change my own mental
state from negative into positive and to look at it as a learning
experience even if it was very challenging or very painful. Use that
to your advantage in moving forward.

He taught me to never stop learning and to develop my own
personality. My personality and leadership style have changed
dramatically since moving to Asia from Australia. One of the things
you realise very early on is that there is no such thing as Asia – we

have offices in China, Japan, Malaysia and Singapore. The different cultures in each country are challenging in their own unique way; I adopt different approaches when in each country. As they say, we have two ears and one mouth, and we should use them in that proportion. Listening, understanding, encouraging people to voice their opinions and really considering what is being said helped me to increase my self-awareness and to understand the importance of diversity. Australians tend to be very forthright and many times outspoken. Many come to Asia and miss out on all that because we speak out too much and too quickly instead of listening and understanding different perspectives first.

> THE IDEA: Every new role you take on is both a leading and a learning experience and the best way to do so is to listen closely to what your followers have to say.

As the Asia Pacific CEO, how do you manage your schedule? Are there any best practices that you employ?

I try to find a work-life balance, and I think that means working smart and putting the right resources in the structures around so that you don't have to do everything. Apart from family, I also have a lot of interests outside of work. I have a rock band in which I play guitar and sing. I also enjoy scuba diving and skiing, and love my motorcycles.

I try to get out of the office by 6pm, because a lot of staff won't leave the office while the CEO is there. Being out of the office makes it easier for them. My work is not from nine to five, but with mobility I can always work in one way or another. Delegating is also a very important part of achieving a work-life balance, although it can be challenging at times to give away things that you feel you can do better.

THE IDEA: Many companies advocate work-life balance, but leaders need to actively encourage such behaviour and demonstrate it through concrete actions, e.g. leaving on time and actively delegating.

LEADING OTHERS

What makes you a great CEO? What do you think makes a great CEO?

I wouldn't call myself a great CEO. I enjoy what I do and therefore I believe that makes a good leader, but ultimately, it is a team effort. I also don't see leadership as a hierarchy with leaders at the top and the workers at the bottom. Leadership of the business runs through the business, right down to the graduates. If there are influencers in the business, there are leaders in the business. Moving forward sometimes means having to change and disrupt your business, and change management is very difficult. Therefore you need these key influencers in the business to manage and drive that change. This is a very important part of my management style – recognising key influencers in the business as leaders and future leaders and letting them know that they are valued and that they play an important part in the success of the business.

THE IDEA: Getting your message and change initiatives right down to the lower levels requires you to harness the support of key influencers at every level of the organisation. Identify who they are and actively engage them in all your decisions.

What do you do to groom future leaders within your organisation?

We do so on many levels with our professional development structure. Firstly, identifying leaders is critical. We have a strong structure in terms of assessing the performance of everyone in the organisation – formal appraisal happens twice a year, and ongoing conversations regarding performance happen throughout the year. These are then collated at the end of the year into performance rankings based on a set of criteria around values, financial performance for the group and their contributions to the business. This identifies the high performers, who are managed individually.

We then have conversations about their career aspirations, because my job, I strongly believe, is to give everyone an opportunity to advance their career. I organise a "blue wave event" every month in every country, where we have conversations with our high potentials over a meal or drinks to understand their aspirations so that they do not feel stuck in their career. It also allows me to understand the challenges in the business. Communication via e-mails over the last 15 years has almost destroyed one-to-one conversations. I think these are invaluable to understand what is going on in the business. It is also important for individuals in the business who want to feel like they are part of the team to feel that they have a voice.

> THE IDEA: Beyond official meetings with your teams, be sure to have regular split-level meetings (i.e. with your subordinates' subordinates) as well as informal gatherings to elicit feedback from junior levels.

What leadership characteristics do you look for in these high potentials?

Energy, passion and a belief that anything is possible. We aim to create an environment where people feel that the company is willing to try their perhaps unorthodox but innovative ideas. We have a focus on promoting innovation and are trying to push it through the business culture to use it as a competitive advantage. If the company does not focus on innovation, we will become a Nokia or Kodak.

LEADING THE ORGANISATION

Could you share more about the Lend Lease Asia business?

I currently have responsibility for the Lend Lease Asia business, which is 2,000 strong and covers Singapore, Malaysia, Japan and China, but represents only approximately 10% of the global business. Many people were extremely surprised when I asked to be considered for this role. My previous role involved running the Australian business, which is now 70% of the global business and some 11,000 strong, and includes Australia's largest developer and constructor and one of the largest property fund managers.

Was this really the right choice for my career, you might ask? To me, running our Australian business was just that – running a big business – whereas I wanted to build a business, and what better place in the world today to do that than right here in Asia? I was always better at building businesses and saw the opportunity to do so in the region, which had never really been driven as hard to grow as in Australia. I've been here for four years, and it's been a lot of fun, I am absolutely loving it. My learning curve has been wonderful. It's been an amazing disruption for me.

Tell me about a leadership challenge that you've overcome and which showcases leadership at its best.

At the end of the day, any challenge that has been overcome has never been an individual effort. When I talk about the organisation, it's very much a "we". We've had a very difficult situation in Singapore in recent years. We've been here for over 40 years and have an amazing relationship with the Singapore government where they see us as a solution-provider, an innovator that is sustainable and driving the industry forward. We had a burst water pipe at the Jem Shopping Centre, and that burst water pipe resulted in 60,000 litres of water wasted and many damaged shops. That was very challenging for us as an organisation because of the damage to our brand. Our brand is sacrosanct and we do our best to protect it. Fortunately, I think we managed the incident because of the strength of our brand, but it was nonetheless very disheartening to see the brand suffer. Interestingly, I think we came out of the incident much stronger as an organisation.

There was also a collapsed ceiling in a very small part of the mall, and we were asked to close that part of the mall while the rest of the shopping centre would stay open. We have an uncompromising approach to safety, and we declined to do so in order to check every part of the shopping centre. It took us two weeks before we were able to reopen the mall. This caused some brand damage, but safety as always was our first priority.

I think the Singapore government was surprised that we closed the entire mall, but they understood our focus on safety and were supportive of us. It was a challenging period, but there were a lot of lessons learnt and we've applied those lessons.

Sometimes, failure is a part of innovation. You can make a mistake, but you can't make the same mistake twice – that's the worst thing that you can do. At the end of the day, I believe we are a stronger organisation, and we've put a lot of effort into the lessons learnt and how we are going to drive that forward. There was so much strong leadership shown by the organisation that made me feel very proud of the team.

> THE IDEA: The organisation's brand and its principles are sacrosanct and the leader has to do whatever it takes to protect the brand's reputation from being tarnished.

What advice would you give to expatriates coming to Asia to lead organisations?

My advice is to listen, and to be culturally aware and respectful. At the end of the day, you are a guest in someone else's home, and you should behave like one. There is a certain arrogance when you come in, as opposed to humility or an understanding of the quality of talent in Asia. There are 3.5 billion people here in Asia and there is obviously a great depth of amazing talent here. The anchoring bias of wanting to employ somebody like yourself will never allow you to succeed. I have a strong focus on localising this business; having an Australian like myself here is quite disappointing, frankly. After 40 years, this business should be entirely localised – it is after all more Singaporean than many Singaporean businesses.

> THE IDEA: Asia is very diverse, with multiple differences between countries, nationalities and cultures. Leading this region requires cultural awareness and great respect for each individual.

SYLVIA LIM
Chairman
Workers' Party

RESPONSIBILITY TO THE PEOPLE

SYLVIA LIM holds a Bachelor of Laws (Hons) degree from the National University of Singapore and obtained a Master of Laws degree in 1989 from the University of London. She was called to the Singapore Bar in 1991. Her keen interest in criminal justice saw her later enrolling for part-time graduate studies with Michigan State University's School of Criminal Justice in 2009, where she obtained a Master of Science in Criminal Justice in May 2014.

Her career path reflected her key interest areas. In 1991, she joined the Singapore Police Force as a police inspector, where she served for three years. In 1994, she returned to practise law in the private sector where she was active in both civil and criminal litigation. In 1998 to 2011 she was a full-time lecturer with Temasek Polytechnic. Her 12 years at the Polytechnic were spent overseeing adult education as well as teaching and researching in civil and criminal procedure, criminal justice and private security.

Sylvia became a Non-Constituency Member of Parliament (NCMP) after leading a Workers' Party (WP) team to contest Aljunied GRC in the 2006 General Elections and securing 43.9% of the votes cast. In the 2011 General Elections, she was part of the victorious Workers' Party team who contested in Aljunied GRC, achieving the first GRC breakthrough for an opposition team with 54.7% of the votes. She is now the Member of Parliamenr representing the Serangoon division of Aljunied GRC.

Sylvia is currently a Senior Associate at M/s Peter Low LLC, a local law firm.

During the 2001 General Elections when two-thirds of seats were uncontested and the ruling party won 75% of the contested votes, Sylvia was very concerned that the fate of alternative parties in Singapore hung in the balance. She believes strongly that alternative parties have a role in scrutinising government policy constructively and asking for justifications for any laws that will affect the people.

Sylvia loves running outdoors but, due to injury, has turned to a lower-impact exercise regime in the form of cycling, swimming and training in the gym. She also enjoys music in many genres from classical to jazz, and is a supporter of the local arts scene.

LEADING YOURSELF

What are some of your leadership and/or career transitions? How did you end up being the Chairperson of the Workers' Party?

In the course of my working life, I have worked in large organisations as well as in smaller ones. In terms of my leadership roles, the role in the political party Workers' Party (WP) is the most significant. I joined the party in 2001, a time when the party was very short on people and especially leaders. During that time, the 9/11 disaster had just happened, the government had called for snap elections and redrew constituency boundaries barely three weeks before polling day. The opposition parties lacked the time to prepare adequately and because of that, over two-thirds of the seats were not contested – WP only contested in two seats. That made me really angry because I value democracy and did not want the elections to be a farce; I thought that if this political trend were to continue, where would we end up? I thus decided that I had to do my part. I was in my mid-30s then, and since I did not have that many commitments, I could make my own decisions, and went ahead to join the party.

How were you elected as Chairperson of the Workers' Party?

WP was initially led by a very small committee and when I joined, some others and I were inducted into an expanded leadership council. I assumed it was not a unanimous decision, which was totally understandable because some of the veterans had no idea who the new people were. We had to prove ourselves along the way. In 2003 (the year I was elected Chairperson), I was asked to consider the Chairperson position. I was shocked to be considered as I still had not had enough time to earn the trust of many party members, especially the veterans who were probably more comfortable in a language and culture quite different from my own. Nonethless, I took up the challenge; we went through an election at the cadre members' conference in 2003 where I contested the incumbent chairman and was voted in.

How did you convince them that you deserved the Chairperson role and how did you continue to maintain that position, having probably been contested in other elections over the years?

I can't disclose too much about what happened at the 2003 cadre conference but I think it was fair to say that the first time I was voted in was an act of faith on the part of many cadre members. Over the years, I was very conscious of the fact that I needed to work harder, to exceed expectations and to correct some misconceptions from skeptics. I spent quite a lot of time doing groundwork which involved working with the party veterans. Over time, they became comfortable with me and my work with the party took on a life of its own. We hold an election for the Chairperson role every two years and I have been in this position for the past 11 years.

> THE IDEA: Getting "sponsorship" and endorsement
> from the senior members of the team is nearly as
> important as proving your own capability.

Do you have any personal leadership role model? How did he/she influence your leadership style?

Over the years, I have come across certain people or certain things that leaders have said that have stuck in my mind and served as a frame of reference.

For example, there is a picture that was given to me by a Singaporean who came to our Hougang by-election rally in May 2012. He hand-painted a picture of the Song Dynasty lady warrior, Mu Gui Ying (穆桂英), with a message encouraging us to continue with our work because without people like us in other political parties trying to push for the people's rights, citizens would suffer. I was extremely touched by this gesture of support and I always look at the painting to remind myself that I have to keep focused on our cause, given that it is probably going to be a long and difficult battle.

As I got to know Mr Low Thia Khiang over the years, I found that he is a very inspiring leader. The characteristics that struck me about him are that first, he is a very fair person and secondly, he dares to take risks with people. When he sees potential in people, he will give you a task that you might think is beyond you but is actually not. Thirdly, he is also open to new ways of looking at things. I find that these characteristics are important as a leader, especially when you want an organisation to adapt to changing circumstances. It is important that you don't bury your head in the sand and ignore the fact that you need to change.

> THE IDEA: Taking the right bets on your people, assessing their potential and then giving them a stretch assignment is a sure way of testing their true potential.

Recently, Nelson Mandela passed away and I was reading excerpts of his life and the legacy he left behind. He was asked why he could not hate his enemies and how he could sit at the negotiation table with the very people who had incarcerated him on Robben Island for decades. He said, "Hating clouds the mind. It gets in the way of strategy. Leaders cannot afford to hate." I find that very powerful and instructive, because sometimes in the thick of political battles, when your integrity is attacked, the tendency is for you to hate the people who afflict that on you. In those times, I take inspiration from Mr Mandela's words – when you are consumed by these negative emotions, you can't think clearly and it will work to the detriment of your organisation. So I try to forget about these people and remind myself to rise above that and come up with a different strategy.

> THE IDEA: "Hating clouds the mind. It gets in the way of strategy. Leaders cannot afford to hate."
> – Nelson Mandela

One final thing that inspired me was the TV series *Band of Brothers*, a war drama about comradeship and leadership. The portrayal of one of the company commanders during the war, Captain (later promoted to Major) Richard "Dick" Winters, was very inspiring to me. He was not a loud or aggressive person, but was very competent as a military commander, strong in his mental and physical fitness and was able to lead in an almost understated manner. Yet, in times of uncertainty, he was able to make quick calculations, decisive actions and also to bear the brunt of problems without losing his temper. I found that very admirable and inspiring. So whenever I feel angry, I think of him and it reminds me to respond in measured ways.

> THE IDEA: Coming across as calm and collected in times of crisis instills confidence among your team members and also facilitates better judgement and decision-making.

Do you have any guidelines or principles that you live by as a leader?

I try my best to apply myself in a way that I think would benefit other people and the community at large. That, to me, is very important. I would probably not be happy with any role that doesn't benefit the society at large. For example, I don't think a job that is purely about the bottom line or salary would motivate me or keep me interested. That's why public service sits well with my own values. I feel that what we do needs to have a broader outreach.

> THE IDEA: Leading others based on a strong set of values sets the compass for your followers to always know where the true north is.

What gets you out of bed every day?

A sense of obligation. Now that I am an elected MP, it raises the stakes to a new level. I have obligations to my constituents and to the public at large to put my time and effort into meaningful activities. At the same time, because we have been given the mandate by people voting us in, we have a responsibility to try to grow the party incrementally such that we can become an effective counterweight to the ruling party. That is a big task which requires pioneering thinking; you just can't do day-to-day cruising – you need to constantly think of new capabilities, new partnerships and new synergies.

> THE IDEA: Complacency has no place in a leader's house. Set aside time to think of new capabilities, new partnerships and new synergies.

How do you maintain your energy on a day-to-day basis?

While I have quit full-time teaching, I am still registered to practise law and would handle some cases here and there while finishing up my Masters studies in criminal justice. I find my area of study in criminal justice symbiotic with my parliament work, where I can delve into some of these issues that I now know better and are important for the country. Practising law is also relevant to my current work.

Coming back to your question, I find it much better now as compared to when I was holding a full-time job that had strict reporting hours. Back then, I found it very tough during certain periods of the year. For example, during the budget debate, it was a big commitment to be at the parliament, but at the same time, I also had exams to grade and report on within short time frames. Now that I have chosen a flexible schedule, it is much better for me and I can get more sleep. I am able to manage at the moment and am in fact thinking of embarking on another teaching career on a part-time basis.

Can you think of a time during your life and/or career where you took a fall? How did you pick yourself up?

No particular "fall" sticks in mind, but there were certainly bad days. For example, bad days could be not performing as well as you thought you should have in parliament or not being able to react well to something unexpected during the session. Although certain things are part and parcel of the job, such as being scolded by a resident, there will be times where you feel demoralised because you have let yourself or others down.

I always remember what my father used to tell me. He was a lawyer too and used to share some coping strategies with me while I was practising law. When you go to court, you never know what is going to happen. Sometimes you can have a bad judge who gives you a hard time or you may lose a case, but always remember that every court appearance, no matter the outcome, is a learning experience. I found that to be very true; we learn from these things and what is important is your fighting spirit, especially for those of us in the opposition. The fighting spirit is more important than avoiding failure, because one has to take risks. One thus has to stay focused on the long-term view when in this vocation. It is also important to remember the reason why you entered politics in the first place, which keeps you going.

But there are always good days. The public makes it a point to let us know that they appreciate what we are doing. For example, after a heated and personal debate in parliament one day, I had an event at my constituency and many residents turned up to encourage me. Having "cheerleaders" along the way motivates me greatly.

LEADING OTHERS

In your opinion, what makes a good leader?
A leader needs to have a vision that people believe is achievable, and be able to craft a general direction that is well articulated to the people he or she works with to achieve the vision. Otherwise, if we do not know where we are heading, we will not know what to do in times of decision-making. I find a leader's fairness to be important as well. The people you work with need to know that you have some objective criteria for decision making, e.g. what kind of opportunities you give to people, what kind of positions you place them in.

How do you continue to bring new talents into the party and build them up?

First of all, we don't usually go around cold-calling to recruit people; the nature of our work is such that there is nothing we can promise our followers materially. Hence, there has to be something deeper that motivates people to join us. One of the reasons people join us is that they believe in the cause we stand for. Besides believing in the cause, I believe that members should be given the chance to contribute their interests or skills in a particular area. We look at their strengths and give them a role where they can maximise what they are good at. Of course, there can be times where you find that some people don't work well together. It may then be better to put them in roles that don't require as much overlap, such that they can function distinctively and still achieve organisational goals.

THE IDEA: Knowing what motivates your team members, e.g. recognition, autonomy, expert knowledge, team work, etc. helps you as a leader to create the right environment to allow them to contribute in these particular areas.

What is the value of having diversity in teams?

It is important to have teams with members from different backgrounds and with different strengths. If you have a team comprising people of the same background who know each other very well, there is a high tendency to descend into a structured kind of decision-making where you can't think any other way. With people of different backgrounds, you realise there are different perspectives and when you make decisions, they are definitely more rounded and holistic. That is probably one danger that the government has to guard against when they look at whom to put in the cabinet.

For me, I enjoy meeting people who are very different from me, because I find myself learning a lot from them. In our party, we have people from all sorts of backgrounds and we have to try to maintain this diversity.

> THE IDEA: Prevent group-think in your teams by actively recruiting members with diverse backgrounds and strengths. Another way is to designate a "devil's advocate" in meetings whose key role is to raise concerns and questions.

Tell me about a significant leadership challenge during your decade plus of experience in leading the Workers' Party.

One episode was the circumstances that led to the Hougang by-election where we expelled elected MP Yaw Shin Leong from our party due to his alleged misconduct. It was a painful and very difficult decision for all of us that required courage and political judgment. I also had to face the media and the public during that difficult time.

It was clearly a difficult leadership challenge for me as I was worried that the faith that the Hougang residents placed in us may have been eroded. It was a period of uncertainty for everyone in the party and morale was low; there was no guidebook telling me how to lead in this kind of situation.

What did you learn from the experience, as a leader?

I think that people don't expect perfection but they expect you to take responsibility and account for what happened, and at the same time, to also be with them during the bad times.

> THE IDEA: People don't expect perfection in you as a leader but they expect responsibility and accountability for your actions.

In your opinion, how do you bring out the best in people?

Given that ours is a non-profit organisation, it is quite a different thing altogether compared to a typical organisation. If you understand an individual's personal goals and why he or she joined in the first place, and you are able to let the person work towards what he or she hopes to achieve, it would be something very valuable.

For example, we have members who find that they want to contribute to policy development. When you accept something that they are proposing after careful study, file a question or bring up a topic in parliament that relates to what they developed, or better yet, when the government responds in a way that brings about policy changes, they get very motivated. Even in my earlier years when I wasn't an MP and I used to help Mr Low to do his parliamentary work, I was always very happy when something that I drafted was reported.

This is especially so for people who are joining us now; many of them have a desire to try and moderate some of the government's policies and when they see you use their hard work and at least articulate it and have it result in some discussion or change, they have a great sense of satisfaction and achievement.

LEADING THE ORGANISATION

Let's move on to talk about leading organisations through change and complexity. What are some of the top challenges that the party is experiencing?

Increased expectation from both within and from the outside is definitely a big challenge we are facing. From the outside, people may feel now that we have some electoral success, they should be seeing very high levels of performance in parliament or that we should have a stronger contribution in terms of policies. Some people are disappointed in us because they feel that we should have done more. Managing the expectations of people within the party is another aspect. Some members may feel that their roles in the party or some of the projects that the party should be doing need to be more ambitious. Some of these criticisms are valid, but we have to manage and prioritise in terms of our resources and where we put our energy.

At the same time, our role in the system as a whole is also in a state of transition. We still have a very small presence in parliament with less than 10% of the seats. In other countries, we would be seen as a marginalised minority party, but of course, when we look at the course of Singapore's history, it is significant progress made.

As the Chairperson, how are you coping with these challenges? What are some things you have done in response to these challenges?

I find that in times of uncertainty and conflicting expectations, I tend to return to the basics and be true to my vows. I don't really care too much about whether the ruling party or the media understands what we are doing, for example. At the time when I joined the party, one of the important pledges that I made to myself was to use my knowledge from my training and work experience to scrutinise laws that will affect the people. I am still quite focused on that.

What is your vision for leading the Workers' Party?

I don't have a grand vision myself. There are many people hoping that we can get ourselves ready at a faster pace to seriously challenge the ruling party in terms of governing Singapore. It is not as easy as they think and I think governing is a heavy responsibility that needs time and experience to prepare for. Fundamentally, we still want to be a party that the people feel is rational, has the interest of the nation at heart and does not want the government to end up in a gridlock position, but at the same time, to also be an effective check against the government. I find that the role is still important, and it is one that people still support.

You're currently reading a book about frames, perhaps you can talk about them and how they apply to the Workers' Party?

As part of my Masters' studies I am reading *Reframing Organisations* by Lee Bolman and Terrence Deal, which covers four frames to consider when making decisions about organisational change. First of all, *structural*, which involves the architecture of the organisation – how you divide roles, how to integrate the different roles, how information flows, etc. The *human resource* frame uncovers how you actually get the best out of people, whether it is through empowerment, through putting people in the right places, through reward systems or development opportunities. There is also the *political* frame – in an environment where people are competing for resources, how do you navigate these and decide what is the best allocation? The last frame, which I think is the most powerful, is the *symbolic* frame. It means that you have to give people something that they can use as a guiding light to move them to another level. It can be overarching principles, credo, stories or taglines that inspire them to greater heights. It is something very elusive but it also has to have authenticity. These are the four frames that the book recommends leaders use to try and develop their organisations more holistically to get the best out of it. I find that they are useful reminders about the importance of balance.

THE IDEA: Great organisations are supported by the four frames of structures that facilitate decision-making, human resource that brings out the best in their people, political avenues that allow fair advocacy for limited resources, all of which are all tied to the symbolic frame that unites the hearts and minds of the people.

Any final advice for aspiring political leaders?

I think it is important to be genuinely committed to the public's welfare.

MAX LOH
Managing Partner for ASEAN and Singapore
EY

LEADING THE PROFESSION

MAX LOH has overall responsibilities for the operations of EY's (formerly known as Ernst & Young) practices in the ASEAN region. He has over 25 years of experience in providing audit and business advisory services to a broad range of clients in various industries that include technology, food and beverage, construction, manufacturing and trading companies, as well as hotels, financial institutions and government concerns.

Max has been involved as an audit partner with various Singapore Exchange (SGX) listed companies and was responsible for their financial statement audits and internal control reviews. He is also experienced in leading teams of reporting accountants for companies in their listings on the SGX, Hong Kong Stock Exchange and Shenzhen Stock Exchange. These include companies from Malaysia, Taiwan, Indonesia, the Middle East and China. He has also taken on reporting auditor roles in reverse takeover exercises.

In addition, Max has assisted Singapore companies in performing due diligence reviews in connection with their acquisition of companies in China, Singapore, Thailand and Malaysia. He is also experienced in strategic planning, reorganisation and operations improvement projects for various local companies as part of their globalisation and listing efforts.

Max graduated from the National University of Singapore with Honours and is a practicing member of the Institute of Singapore Chartered Accountants. He is a board member and Audit Committee Chair of the Health Sciences Authority, board member and Public Accountants Oversight Committee Member of the Accounting and Corporate Regulatory Authority, board member of Singapore Polytechnic, Exco member and Audit Committee Chair of the Institute of Singapore Chartered Accountants and member of the Appeals Committee for the Council of Estate Agents.

LEADING YOURSELF

Please share with me your career transitions leading up to your current roles.

I joined the profession after graduating from the National University of Singapore, where I studied accountancy. I was previously from the science stream and moved to accountancy mainly because I wanted to have a professional career. After graduating, I joined Arthur Andersen in 1986, which was then one of the eight premier accountancy firms. I stayed there for 10 years, where I made partner. After which I was tasked to do various things, in which I wasn't so specialised. I did auditing, tax, business structuring and a bit of strategy.

There was benefit in engaging on a multitude of projects. I felt that I became a better business person as I could look at issues from multiple business perspectives. In 1996 I became a partner. I then led the Initial Public Offering (IPO) practice in Andersen as we built an IPO business. Many entrepreneurial companies were growing overseas; globalising and tapping the capital markets and so I was put in charge of helping these companies. There was a good "golden period" as many companies were getting listed. I was fairly successful and I enjoyed myself because I had always wanted to work with entrepreneurs. They bring to the table a different set of values, energy and enthusiasm that rubs off on you and makes it very exciting. Andersen then ran into problems with the Enron situation in 2002. With the collapse of Andersen, we had to find a new "home". Most of the practices in Asia-Pacific merged with Ernst & Young in 2002 and I have been here ever since. In 2011, I took on the role as the Singapore country head as well as the managing partner for ASEAN. So I now look after the Southeast Asian countries, which is very exciting because of the varying markets, immense economic potential, differences in culture, values and opportunities.

What is your definition of a leader?
Firstly, it is always leadership by example. You have to go into the trenches to make your people also want to go into the trenches. That is not to say don't delegate and do everything yourself. But you have to demonstrate that to the troops. So when you want to ask people to do certain things, such as embarking on a certain strategy or a different direction, you have to live it and make sure it works before people will follow you. I take it upon myself as the leader to say "let's charge", and there I am at the front of the spear.

Secondly, leadership is different from management in that you have to make the right decisions and not just execute strategies that have already been determined. Tough decisions are what leaders make for the benefit of the firm. In contrast, management is more about executing an existing strategy and plan and making sure everybody toes the line. But leadership is more than that. It is about driving change, which is always difficult. It is easy to say, "Let's just continue the things we have been doing, we have been successful". I think that the only people who survive and thrive are those who are most responsive to change. So we have to continually challenge ourselves to innovate, to be productive, to add value to our clients and drive that within the organisation. But people don't like change. There are people in our organisation who have been here for 35 years and they'll ask, "Change? Haven't I been doing it right?" I will say, "Yes, you have been, but we can do it better". Leadership is about the conviction and competence to drive change and making sure that everybody follows. They might not like it all the time but they must see that it is the right way to go. That is an important aspect of leadership.

> THE IDEA: Leaders are creators of change and to lead change, the leader needs to do so by example.

Did you have role models, and what did you learn from them in terms of leadership lessons?

I think all of us who have "grown up" in a professional services firm have benefited from having coaches and mentors who take it upon themselves to make you successful. I premise my success in being able to develop and find a successor who can do even better. I think that is an important part of leadership – it is not just about what happens when you are there, but what happens after you leave.

I have had several role models who have guided and mentored me and who exhibit passion in everything that they do. I learnt from them the importance of "thinking straight and talking straight", to be a leader who is clear-minded and candid. This resonates with the nature of our profession. When we come across difficult problems, we cannot shy away from them. We have to be independent and objective and communicate clearly to our clients why a particular position is the right one.

I am also reminded of a manager I had when I was a first-year staff. He had an incredible work ethic. He might have had many things on his table but he would finish his work very efficiently and his desk would be clean at the end of the day, no matter what came his way. That struck me as something that we should emulate or strive to achieve.

When I was a manager, I had various partners who took it upon themselves to nurture me. This is important because we look upon our senior people as role models. We also need to have diverse talent to make this organisation successful. We always question if a particular person is successful because he or she is technically competent, or has great communication skills or the right attitude. These are the qualities that we learnt from our seniors. We are all different, but I think the key values and the key traits are what inspired us.

There was a particular partner who took it upon himself to guide me more closely. Our leverage ratio is usually about one partner to many people so I was gratified that he took a personal interest in me. It is therefore important to continue this tradition.

Another example of a role model was a leader who tasked me with taking on this role. I was the IPO leader then and I thought that there would be an intermediate position before progressing to the position of regional managing partner. I was also doing pretty well as a line partner; my clients liked me and I liked working with clients. I knew that when I took on this role that I would be doing less client work, which I love, and more management, so I had a conversation with the leader about it. I told him that I was actually quite happy with what I was doing, but I understood if the firm needed me to step up. What convinced me was really the comment that "We are ambitious for you because we see that you can and you have the potential to do this."

> THE IDEA: Your faith and confidence in your follower can have a great catalytic effect on their motivation to succeed in an expanded role.

Could you share with me some leadership principles that you believe in and live by?

I think it is important to have the basic values about what it means to be a professional. Once you get the basics right, it is then about applying yourself to various situations and the things you want to achieve. Enthusiasm and drive are key; we definitely cannot lose our passion for client service because in our business, clients are our livelihood.

In our industry, there are clients on the demand side, and the people on the supply side. The two are balanced on a seesaw with the important fulcrum of quality in everything that we do. To me, leadership on the client side involves thinking about how we can become more relevant to the market and therefore being exceptional in client service, connectivity and delivering value-added work. In terms of the people, we are all role models. Our people look up to us to see what we are doing. EY now has close to 200,000 people worldwide. It is a huge organisation. And with size comes the risk of lack of nimbleness and flexibility. We need to continue to innovate and try new things and enable change management in the process.

So for example, we're continually innovating to empower our people to achieve work-life integration, through building a workplace of the future where people work anytime and from any place in a refreshed physical work environment.

Such changes are important but not easy. It is vital for us to progress to the next level, or risk being stuck in a rut of complacency. For example, as an auditor in our organisation, you audit the books every year. You gain a bit of experience as the year passes, but then what? Do you take the financial statements the following year and audit them again? That cannot and should not be the case. If so, the organisation will never grow. So we always have to come up with new services and identify new client needs so that we can bring our expertise to bear. There are many competent people within our organisation; we just need to translate their abilities into service offerings for our clients. It is important that our clients see a value in that.

> THE IDEA: Being an effective leader means balancing the seesaw of conflicting needs, meeting client demands on one side and people constraints on the other side, with "quality" as the fulcrum.

Think of your own development as a leader. What are one or two highlights in terms of how you developed yourself, and what were your best developmental opportunities?

I think the important thing to note is that opportunities don't happen by themselves, you have to grab them. When I was much younger, I always took advantage of the opportunities that I saw. So even though I am an accountant by training, I would take on a consulting project because I felt that I could grow my skillsets in the process. Being involved in a broad spectrum of projects not only makes you a better business person, it also builds up your technical skills. So I think grabbing the opportunities, as opposed to waiting for them to happen, is a very important part of developing yourself. Find role models to emulate, people whom you feel are doing the right things and exhibiting the right values, but don't just copy their behaviours wholesale. Determine which of their traits and attitudes are best suited to your own style.

> THE IDEA: Broadening your skillsets and volunteering for projects outside of your work scope prepares you for general management. Aligning yourself with role models instills crucial leadership habits.

I see it as being similar to grafting; you cut the best part and graft it to yourself.

But you still have to add the right fertiliser and care for it to ensure that the fruit is better than the previous crop. I am a firm believer in coaching and mentoring. If you feel that there is a different style or perspective that suits you, that is fine, it is not a one-size-fits-all approach. But when you run ideas past other people, their diverse perspectives enable you to broaden your vision and make better decisions. Even though I am a leader of the ASEAN practice, I regularly consult with others because I don't have all the answers and no one can do it alone. I always tell my people that the strength of EY is in the collective wisdom of all its partners and people.

> THE IDEA: Problems are often complex and multi-faceted. The leader needs to harness collective wisdom and having done so, be decisive in making a call.

How do you see the issue of work–life integration?

It is important to have work-life integration, but I always emphasize that a professional is not someone who says work is an 8am to 5pm affair. Does it mean that a policeman is no longer on the job if he sees something amiss after 5pm? No. I have a younger brother who is a doctor. We could be playing golf together and at the second hole he would say, "I have to go, I must attend to a patient." I am not saying that you should work 24 hours a day, but a professional is one who is dedicated to his craft and is flexible. You may rest once your job is done, but it is never defined by a time frame.

A true professional is someone who wants to be the best that they can be in their craft, and that includes technical competence, the way you communicate with clients and other colleagues, the way you manage the expectations of stakeholders that might include regulators, the government, clients, other business people and even competitors. Everyone in EY is a professional and in order to be successful, they have to make a difference. How can you make a difference? How can you differentiate yourself from the next person? Do things that make you stand out, and grab the opportunities that come along to grow and develop further in a big organisation.

> THE IDEA: Build yourself as a leader and professional at the same time, which means honing your technical competence, communication and presentation skills and stakeholder management capabilities to be an all rounder.

LEADING OTHERS

What do you look for when building a power team?

We have leadership positions in our service lines (e.g. audit, tax, advisory, transactions) and market segments. These leaders report to me because we want to make sure that they are all connected and aligned, and that we bring the best resources to our clients, irrespective of service lines and geographies.

When building a team, we look at the following factors:

1. They must be good executors and excellent at managing projects, clients and people.

2. It is important that they are builders. First, they have to be "people builders" because our business is about people. There is always a need for succession planning. Success should be measured on how you have groomed people who are ready to step into your position and do even better than you. Next, they must be a "business builder". That is, being able to identify the right resources, capabilities and expertise to build the organisation so that we can resolve even more issues on a global scale.

3. The last one is what I call the "market builder". We have to build the market. Without the market, you may have the best people in the world but you are not going to excel. "Market building" involves connectivity with clients, building relationships based on doing the right thing, etc. It all relates to two important things: the business and the people. We need to be able to show the market that we are the best at what we do. Every business is competitive – I always ask myself why clients should choose EY. There had better be many reasons why, or else it will always come down to price each time we go for a competitive bid. An organisation that fights on price alone is unlikely to succeed.

So I think the leadership has to be united and have a shared vision. I have no qualms in bringing in the right talent or leader who is able to engage the market and drive value for the firm, and paying the person the right remuneration to do so. We have to recognise that different people have different strengths. Some are good at executing projects, others are technically superb and knowledgeable in a particular subject matter, while others are great at client service. The key, I think, is being able to identify the strengths in different people and deploying them in the right places, empowering them and motivating them to work together to do the best they can.

THE IDEA: Building a strong team of fellow leaders requires a diverse portfolio of executors together with people and market builders.

Do you have any real-life examples of such?

I spend a lot of time trying to engage partners and people, particularly on how we can work together to bring value to the client. Every partner has to get past the thought that a particular client is *theirs*. No, it is the firm's client – you are just handling the account.

You must be able to bring everybody together, regardless of where they reside and whether they have sector expertise. For example, if a client is in the gaming sector, I have to bring in people from Las Vegas because they have a longer history with the industry and are the experts. When I was a young auditor, auditing was fairly straightforward. Now, in order to complete a good audit, you need to have a valuation expert because many things are determined by "fair value". You now need to have a derivatives expert as many corporations (not just banks) engage in risk management via financial instruments. You also need to have controls experts and analytics experts because data analytics is now critical to businesses. So auditing is no longer a one-dimensional job. Pool everybody together and set the right benchmarks to demonstrate that without teamwork, you will not be successful.

> THE IDEA: Think beyond your own silos and stretch beyond functions and geographies to pool the best talent possible to meet clients' needs.

With so much complex information, how do you synthesise everything and make decisions for yourself?

Of course, I don't do it alone. I consult my team and take in all the information before looking at the entire picture. Sometimes, we are faced with limitations. For example, we are not unlimited in our capacity to invest. In such situations, prioritisation is key as we may not be able to do everything at the same time. Whether that is leadership or management, we just have to make sure that we set the right priorities and do the right thing at the right time. We'll get round to everything, but perhaps not all at once.

You talked about succession planning and grooming of partners and leaders. What are some things that EY does well in these aspects?

I think it is still a work in progress, although we have made great progress in this regard. We look at our partners and use a "nine box model" to measure their potential and effectiveness and decide where they reside in the model. For the people who sit on the upper right of the box, we have learning and development programmes and assign external coaches to help them develop their potential. We actually replicate this with the senior managers. Before they become partners, we have what is called the "next generation programme" where senior managers who have the potential to become partners go through specialised programmes that equip them with management and leadership skills and give them opportunities to mingle with leadership because that is where you learn. Succession planning is so important for us because none of us are going to be here forever.

How do you pick your leaders?

I always tell my leaders not to have an unconscious bias when recommending potential partners for promotion or high performers to me. Please don't just identify people who are of the same mould as you. If so, EY would be made up of a bunch of robots, just doing the same things over and over again. I make it a point to take into consideration gender diversity, different nationalities and skillsets when we look at promotions to ensure diversity of knowledge, thought and vision. If clients are just as diverse, why would they pay for conventional thinking?

> THE IDEA: Resist the impulse to choose leaders in your likeness and consider possible biases regarding your choices in people. Seek out complementary skillsets rather than complimentary ones!

Tell me about a challenge at EY that showcased you as a leader.

Recently, we embarked on a project involving the workplace of the future, which means not having fixed desks and using technology to enhance the work experience. We have revolutionised our audit methodology so people already do audits using technology. With technology, thick files are a thing of the past. We are also able to access files even if we are on an engagement elsewhere. So partners can now review work anywhere and anytime using technology that we have invested in. That gives us an opportunity to change the way we work. There is now a FlexPro programme where our people are empowered to choose where, when and how they work, and such flexibility keeps our people happy and motivated. I always emphasise that it isn't about being present, but about outcomes. As long as you achieve the objective.

> THE IDEA: To encourage work-life balance, leaders should start placing an emphasis on ROWE (Results Only Work Environments) instead of mere face-time from their staff.

Was there resistance to your proposed changes?

As with any change, resistance is to be expected. For example, there are concerns that people would not be working while out of the office and that their team leaders can't keep track of them. For me, it is about a trust-based and a collaborative environment. There will always be people who will feel uncomfortable and ask why you are driving such a change. I replied that it was the right and important thing to do. I am not kicking this can down the road until the next leader takes over because I am spending money to get this done and I have to be accountable and live by it.

How do you handle resistance and ensure that your team transitions smoothly?

It involves constant communication and engaging with people to let them see the benefits of the changes. When we first started using technology, there were many people who still wanted to have printed work papers because they had been doing so for years and were comfortable with it. We had to convince them that change was here to stay and that they had to embrace it. We have to constantly try to make progress. You must have the belief and the determination to get things done and to convince your stakeholders. And it has turned out well so far. At the end of the day, when people see the reason behind it, they will jump on to the bandwagon.

Another strategy to handle detractors is having full transparency. We need to constantly engage with our people and be as transparent as possible – where we are going? What are we doing? Why are we doing this? How does it benefit them? Why are they also going to be successful as we embark on this? We need to empower people because they are all professionals. Of course, we do have governance to make sure that things are done properly and we constantly get feedback from clients on how we are doing. But the value of EY lies in its brand, and the brand lies with its people. It is all interlinked. If our people are not up to scratch, we lose points from our brand, if our people are good, clients love their experience with us, we get the job done and drive value-added solutions, and gain points for the brand.

THE IDEA: Engage in constant communication and transparency to help team members successfully transition through change.

Leaders are sometimes defined by learning lessons as much as their successes. What are some of the challenges that you have experienced and what have you learnt from them?

When I was younger, I was a very enthusiastic market builder and sometimes neglected the people engagement side of things. Our work is not about growing market share all the time and I learnt that it is important to take a step back and evaluate if our people are engaged. As you build a practice, you must make sure that your people are also enjoying the process. At the end of the day, it is not just about success – the welfare of the entire firm needs to be taken care of.

Like the analogy of driving a car but being very careful not to burn the engine?

The key lesson from this would be that I want to drive things fast, but to also build this fantastic engine. And that's what we have been doing more aggressively over the past couple of years – making sure that our engine is bigger, broader and has more capabilities before we race.

LEADING THE ORGANISATION

Tell me about your work with EY in the region.

We have about 14,000 people across most of the markets in Southeast Asia, including Sri Lanka and Guam. It is a fast-growing region; people are optimistic, the formation of the ASEAN Economic Committee in 2015 bodes very well for us because foreign direct investors are now looking at a region of more than 600 million people with a growing middle class and better consumer spending power. That said, there are bound to be risks such as geo-political tension and diversity in terms of different cultures and languages.

How do you manage a region as diverse as Asia?

We need to have strong practices in each country, and have a level of expertise that can cut across and work in all geographies. We are building the business out of specific areas, mainly in Singapore because there is a lot of talent here and it's a very liveable city. We have moved many of our businesses here because Singapore has strengths in the financial sector, oil and gas, as well as analytics. However, the market in Singapore is too small, so our professionals actively explore projects or opportunities in the region. This "hub and spoke" model works well for us because it does not make sense to fully build capabilities in all countries.

How do you view the growth prospects in this region?

Many ASEAN countries are doing pretty well. The Philippines has been growing well, and after the elections in Indonesia, there is now certainty in terms of the political leadership with President Joko Widodo. Singapore and Malaysia have always been steady markets. Thailand is still going through flux. Vietnam has a lot of market potential, although I think they have to undergo a lot of reform and be braver in terms of getting things done. But generally, the market outlook for the region is pretty bullish, and I have a mandate to make sure that we invest in and continue to grow the ASEAN practice.

What is your five-year vision and strategy for building the business in the region?

We have a global strategy that underpins our single purpose of building a better working world. As a region, we have ambitious growth plans. We want to be a very strong multi-disciplinary professional services organisation. When people look at the "big four" accounting firms, they associate EY with auditors. Yet, only 50% of our business involves auditing and in some countries, it is less than 50%. So when we say multi-disciplinary, what other areas are we referring to? The consulting sector is a big area for us. We are investing in areas such as supply-chain management to help companies improve their performance and looking at IT strategies, cyber security, digital analytics and other things that the C-Suite would think about. We are also looking into areas such as risk management, tax advisory and business transformations.

What are the key things that you will focus on?

These areas that we have identified are relevant to our business. We don't sell ice to eskimos. First, you have to identify what your clients and their businesses need. Then you look at what you can offer. So we look at the areas in which our clients need services, identify the megatrends and where businesses are headed and make sure we have the relevant skill sets to support them. The growth plans for ASEAN are quite bullish. We are investing heavily in building up our advisory capabilities. We are also looking at the transactional side of things – helping companies look at their capital agenda and how they invest, divest, balance their portfolios, as well as their strategies on how to move forward in this ever complex world. So I would say that the consulting part of our business is a big area of focus because we feel that our clients really value that.

> THE IDEA: Focus less on the products you are selling and instead regularly evaluate the areas in which your clients need services, identify megatrends and where businesses are headed and make sure you have the relevant skill sets to support them.

What are the prospects of auditing and how do you stay ahead of the market?

Auditing will always be our bread and butter, because companies need their books to be audited. Companies always want to go public and tap the capital markets for fund raising, and we need to make sure that financial statements are timely and relevant so that investors can make the right decisions. To stay ahead of the curve, we focus on areas that add value to the audit, for example, adding sector expertise and perspectives or using analytics to draw insights. Essentially, we use our people's existing skill sets and supplement them with new relevant skill sets to make sure that we lead in this space. That can also tie back to leadership – the ability to look forward, identify opportunities and talent and pull them all together.

As a leader for EY's ASEAN business, do you have any advice in terms of balancing the region's concerns with that of the global organisation and making sure that the voice of the region is heard?

As the regional managing partner for ASEAN, I sit on EY's global practice group. The regional managing partners do come together to talk through our strategy and what the global organisation wants to do and how this fits the local region. We have robust discussions during these meetings, which I think the global organisation is very receptive towards.

How are decisions made in this global practice group?

We have three strategic pillars at EY and one of them is focused on strengthening our global organisation, and empowering the local market. We want to have a very strong core in the global organisation that drives strategy and connect us all. But we also want to make sure that the local regions are empowered to adapt these strategies to fit their own purposes.

How do you balance potential conflicts in priorities between these pillars in practice?

There will sometimes be tension, because when you want to deviate from a structured position, there is always the question of why. It is not a one-size-fits all strategy, but I think it is a healthy tension – if everyone has the same view, how can we improve? If we can't offer new insights to our clients, we are not relevant. How can we be insightful? When doing a tax return, don't just tick the boxes. Tell the client what the risks are. Tell the client what areas they can improve on to minimise taxes in a proper, legal manner. How can they better structure their transactions? That's value-adding and is what will keep clients coming back to us because we have either saved them money, or prevented them from falling into a pit. Either way, it's a plus.

> THE IDEA: A leader in the knowledge-based industry needs to constantly push beyond conventional excellent service and instead inspire his team to provide clients with fresh insights.

What is your next peak as a leader?

I am already overseeing a very exciting region, which I am thankful for, and humbled that the global leadership thinks I am the right person for the job. I need to deliver on this, of course. There are many challenges in many countries and we need to deliver on our aspirations, not just in terms of financial targets, but in terms of being the most attractive employer.

I want EY to be the best place to work in because people will feel empowered and motivated. I want to have the best brand and to be a market leader... the list could go on. I'm on a transformation journey to achieve all of that – I haven't thought beyond that or my next peak – till I feel I'm satisfied with what I sought to achieve.

What is your final word of advice for a young graduate hoping to become a manager or partner and to one day succeed you as the region's managing partner for EY?
You must have the right attitude, and then the right aptitude to want to achieve. I think you can build up aptitude with experience. You also need connectivity and communication – being able to operate in and as a team, because no one person is able to resolve things alone in today's complex world.

ARNOUD DE MEYER
President
Singapore Management University

LEADING COLLABORATIVELY

PROFESSOR DE MEYER is the fourth president of the Singapore
Management University (SMU). Previously, he was Director of
Judge Business School at the University of Cambridge, where
he was Professor of Management Studies and Fellow of Jesus
College. He was associated with INSEAD for 23 years, during
which he held various senior academic and administrative
positions, including founding Dean of INSEAD's Asia Campus
in Singapore.

Professor De Meyer has a Master of Science in Electrical
Engineering, as well as an MBA and PhD in Management from
the University of Ghent in Belgium. He also pursued his studies
as a visiting scholar at the Sloan School of Management,
Massachusetts Institute of Technology (USA). His research
interests are in manufacturing and technology strategy,

the implementation of new manufacturing technologies, the management of R&D, how innovation can be managed more effectively, project management under conditions of high uncertainty, management and innovation in Asia, the globalisation of Asian firms, the management of novel projects and e-readiness in Europe. His works are published widely in academic journals and books.

Professor De Meyer has been a consultant to a number of companies throughout Europe and Asia. He was a member of the Singapore Economic Review Committee (2002–2003), board member of the Infocomm Development Authority (2000–2003) and Sentosa Island Corporation (2001–2002). He is currently an external director of Dassault Systèmes SA (France), as well as a board member of the National Research Foundation, Singapore International Chamber of Commerce, Temasek Management Services and Singapore Symphonia Company Limited. He is on the International Advisory Committee of the School of Business, Renmin University of China, as well as a member of the Academic Council of China Europe International Business School.

LEADING YOURSELF

How did you become the President of the Singapore Management University?

As an academic, I did not start my career with the ambition of being a leader. After a short time in the industry as an engineer, I went to graduate school to pursue a PhD. When I graduated, I looked for a job in academia. When I look back at my career, every step I took made a lot of sense at the time but it was not with a vision of becoming the president of a university. At INSEAD, and subsequently at Cambridge, I took on some management responsibilities, which I did reasonably well. In fact, I hadn't even heard of Singapore when I graduated as an engineer in 1976. Therefore, I cannot say that I followed a real purposeful path, but I enjoyed what I was doing at every stage of my life.

Do you have any leadership role models?

I am an academic, so I am influenced by what academic research tells about leadership. That said, there are two individuals who have influenced me, both of whom I have worked closely with. One is the former dean of INSEAD, António Borges, who taught me two things. First, be a master of your own diary. As a leader, many people will want your time and attention. It is important to stay in charge of your own time or you will be drawn away from what you really have to do. Second, as a leader you need a vision and a clear strategy to achieve that vision. You have to be very clear about your strategy and communicate that strategy clearly. Another leader I learnt a lot from is the former vice-chancellor of Cambridge, Allison Richard. From Allison, I learnt that as a leader you can't do too much. For instance, if you start a programme wanting to do 50 things, you will inevitably fail. I remember her telling me that in my five-year term, it would require one year of learning the role and four years to do the job, during which I could only achieve three things each year. I learnt that it is important to limit yourself to what you can achieve and put all your resources into achieving them. These are the three things I have learnt and applied clearly in my life.

> THE IDEA: Focus on three major things you want to achieve every year and be cautious not to divert your energy to doing too much things at the expense of achieving none of them.

During your own leadership journey, have you come up with your own leadership principles?

Yes. I strongly believe that leadership is situational. While I may be a good leader for an academic organisation, I may not necessarily be a good leader, for example, in a consumer goods business. I have developed for myself what I call "collaborative leadership". It is the idea that leading people is to get things done through a community of people and not by control. This is especially important in a university setting, where you have a large group of very intelligent people with strong personalities. Therefore, a good leader should be the "first amongst peers", rather than a leader on top of an organisation. This form of leadership requires a lot of listening, convincing and making sure that people adhere to and buy into your vision for the organisation, while remaining flexible to changing circumstances. While collaborative leadership is ideal, there may be some disadvantages if you are not careful. For instance, listening to others may lead to procrastination and being flexible may result in a lack of clarity of purpose in terms of your aims and vision. So there is a fine line between the pros and cons of collaborative leadership, but it is something I believe in.

THE IDEA: More often than not, leaders tend to lead intellectual equals with strong personalities. In such cases, adopting a form of "collaborative leadership" which involves consensus building and flexibility regarding changing circumstances can build trust and respect among peers.

Tell me about a day in your life as a leader at SMU.

Forty per cent of my time is spent on representing the organisation. Some might say that it is a waste of time to meet business partners and government representatives and be present at events that students organise. However, I find that it is important to put a face to an organisation so that people can identify with the organisation. The rest of my time is spent on three things. First, strategy – most of my collaborators, for good reasons, are completely absorbed by short-term operational issues. My role is to ensure that the organisation keeps thinking long-term. Second, integrating different parts of the university. There is a need to ensure that different parts, functions and schools keep talking to each other and stimulate integration in the organisation. Third, ensuring the financial stability of SMU. As they say, the buck stops with the President or the CEO, so financial stability is something I spend a lot of my time on.

What gets you out of bed every day?

I like my job. I like to interact with students. I have the freedom in my life to do what I like to do. If the day comes where I do not like what I am doing, I can always fall back to being an academic.

How do you keep yourself energised?

I do so by keeping a balance between the time I spend on my private life and my professional life. I work long days, but I do take time off. I also have the ability to switch off completely from my professional life. I sleep well, partially because I am able to compartmentalise my professional and personal life and switch between them quite well. I had an Organisational Behaviour teacher who taught me that because time is limited, it is important to balance your time in three areas: work, family and relationships with friends, and your passions. That balance may change over the course of your life, but it is important to keep in mind that a human being needs to have those three things.

> THE IDEA: As a leader, stress is a constant feature of life. Being able to compartmentalise between professional and personal life and balancing the three areas of work, relationships and passions ensures career longevity.

What are some of the qualities that make a good leader?

When you reach a certain level in an organisation, you are obviously there because of your strengths. However, you are bound to have weaknesses. Therefore, to be a good leader, I must first find people with strengths, but who can also compensate for my weaknesses as well as complement each other's strengths. Secondly, leading a team at this level involves members with strong personalities. A good leader is one who can enable the team to interact and appreciate each other's strengths as well as their individual weaknesses. Thirdly, as a leader I have to be conscious of the way I interact with the people I lead. If, through my body language for example, I show a person that I do not appreciate him or her, it may become self-fulfilling. That is why I am extremely conscious of the way I communicate, which includes my body language.

> THE IDEA: A leader is constantly being noticed by his/her followers and judged not just by what he or she says, but also in terms of body language.

LEADING OTHERS

How do you bring out the best in the team that you work with at SMU?

This first relates to what we have discussed, that is to avoid setting them up to fail. Instead, I try to provide positive enforcement to bring out their best. The second point is to have clear objectives, and the third is to give a lot of freedom to allow the team to achieve those objectives. I work with intelligent and hardworking people; if I am clear and able to communicate what I want to achieve with this university, I do not need tell them how and what to do. I think this is the best way to achieve the best out of people.

Tell me about a time where you had to overcome a leadership challenge.

The first instance happened 15 years ago when I had the role of initiating INSEAD in Singapore. There was some resistance by the faculty in France, some of whom were friends and colleagues I had worked with for many years. While I did not have any problems with the disagreements they had professionally, some disagreements became personal in nature, which was difficult to deal with. To overcome that, I could only do my best to persuade and convince them. As a leader, one needs to have a thick skin and be willing to accept the personal attacks as a form of managerial challenge.

Another example would be the instances when I do not get the results I want. As an academic, I have grown used to criticism, through the criticisms I receive from blind reviews when I submit papers for publications. Academics will be familiar with the experience of receiving criticism even though he or she may have tried their best. However, these criticisms do eventually lead to better papers. Likewise, I have used the publication process as an analogy to overcome challenges such as not getting the results I want.

THE IDEA: A leader cannot let their ego get in the
way. Treat disagreements and criticism as a form of
managerial challenge to improve upon ideas.

LEADING THE ORGANISATION

Tell me about SMU, the organisation that you are currently leading.

SMU has a pool of 1,100 employees, of which 350 are faculty members. We probably have a higher ratio of support personnel to professionals compared to a typical organisation such as a bank or a law firm. That is because we have 8,500 students who are, to some extent, our product in that we educate them before handing them to companies who recruit them. They are also, to some extent, our customers in that we have to provide them with a service. There is also an element of pastoral care that is needed, although most are mature and independent. As an organisation it is a little strange in the sense that it is a professional organisation, but at the same time you have an entire group of students with you for four years.

What would you say are the top challenges facing this multi-faceted organisation?

There are four points to that. First, universities are by definition slow-moving organisations. Since the university functions in a cyclical manner in terms of students coming in each year, a lot of changes and experiments you make can only be done once a year. In some cases, you will only be able to see results much later. In that sense, it is very different from other fast-moving organisations such as consumer goods, consulting and banking, where you have to react very quickly.

The second challenge is to find a way to adjust our business model, as a university, to suit the 21st century. I think that the traditional, disciplined-based university with research as its primary task and the way it functioned independently from society is now obsolete. There is also a challenge in our commitment to lifelong learning. We used to only take in students between the ages of 18 and 28, but the question is how do we commit ourselves to lifelong learning in a knowledge-based society where one does not stop learning at 28.

Third, with technology having a huge impact in society, we have to rethink the ways in which we are teaching. The university used to have a monopoly of information as well as the brightest minds. With today's technology, you do not necessarily have to go to a university to learn or seek knowledge. Therefore, the advancement of technology requires us to think very hard about what learning involves and how we as faculty members react to that. Fourth, the competitive landscape of the university is changing; we are no longer national in nature and have to react to the effects of globalisation.

What are some things that you are doing to cope with these challenges?

First, I believe we need to do a lot more interdisciplinary research on a larger scale by bringing good people together, which requires incentives. Second, we need to invest heavily on studying our pedagogical model, not just in terms of technology, but also a change in attitudes of our students. Students accept far less authority than they used to – and for a good reason – our authority was based on the fact that the faculty knew things and the students didn't. That basis of authority has disappeared, since students know a lot more now. That is why we need to invest in "project-based learning", which is a more experiential type of learning, and think of ways to change our pedagogical methods. Third, we need to be much more open to society. We are a city university, and we have the big advantage of being in the middle of the city. We are actually open to professionals and business people, and I hope people always feel welcome at the university. We probably need to be more open to the community at large, and be more of an open city university. These are the three things I think we should do a lot more of. Of course, there are other things we need to do such as good research, investing in our alumni and being a specialist in Asia, but you will hear the same things from our counterparts at NUS and NTU. To differentiate ourselves we need to be an open university, to engage in multidisciplinary research and reinvent our pedagogical methods.

What is the legacy you would like to leave at SMU?

SMU is a young university and I think our future is very bright. Even if I am no longer here and with others managing this institution, our opportunity is to be a leading university in the broad area of social sciences, management and Information technology. By social sciences, I mean in the European tradition of anything that is not stamped with either "science", "engineering" or "medical research", etc. I think we have the opportunity to become a leading research-driven social sciences university in Asia. That is the ambition and potential of SMU.

As a leader, I see myself more as a custodian and a guide, entrusted with the institution for a number of years. As a guide, I am able to steer the institution in the right direction, or perhaps speed up the evolution, but I believe that the potential of the university does not lie with me, but with all the people here – the students, alumni and the partners of the university. In terms of legacy, I do not think I am in a position where I am required to make radical changes, but I hope to be associated with guiding the university in such way that we are able to achieve things a little faster.

THE IDEA: The leader does not own the institution but serves as a guide to steer it in the right direction and towards a better vision.

What is your advice for someone in your field, perhaps an academic aspiring to be Dean or even President of a university?

Firstly, do the things you like to do. While there were some difficult moments, I would say that the majority of things I have done over my lifetime are things I like to do. To illustrate: I chose an academic career, and I chose to be a leader in an academic institution. During my career, I have been asked if I was interested in alternate careers in management consulting or some other non-educational field. However, I have always stayed in academia because I still continue to publish, research and teach. I have kept myself alive as an academic because I do the things I like. And so my first advice would be to try to fill your days with things that you are passionate about.

Leadership is about achieving *change* positively for the organisation through a community of people. It is different from the concept of management, which is concerned with the use of skills and capabilities to handle complexities. My second advice would be that if you really want to lead, you need the guts to change things.

The third advice would be to have a thick skin.

JACK SIM
Founder
World Toilet Organisation

SERVANT LEADERSHIP

Widely known as "Mr Toilet", JACK SIM broke the global taboo surrounding toilets and sanitation by bringing the agenda into the global media spotlight with his unique mix of humour and serious facts since 2001.

Born in poverty in 1957, Jack started his first business at age 24, eventually founding 16 businesses ranging from building materials trading, manufacturing, franchising, real estate development and building the Australian International School in Singapore. After attaining financial independence at the age of 40 as a businessman, he decided to quit the rat-race to devote the rest of his life to social work. Some of his achievements include:

- 1998: Founded the Restroom Association of Singapore.
- 2001: Founded World Toilet Organisation (WTO) as a global network and service platform for toilet

associations to promote sound sanitation and public health policies.

- 2004: Awarded the inaugural Singapore Green Plan Award by Singapore's National Environment Agency for contributions to the environment.
- 2005: Founded the World Toilet College. Successfully lobbied and changed Singapore's building codes to allow more cubicles in ladies' restrooms. The US Congress passed a similar law in 2010.
- 2006: Awarded Social Entrepreneur of the Year by Schwab Foundation of Switzerland and became a Schwab Fellow of the World Economic Forum.
- 2008: Appointed to the World Economic Forum's Global Agenda Council for Water Security and Social Entrepreneurship. *Time* magazine named him Hero of the Environment.
- 2009: Named Asian of the Year by Channel NewsAsia.
- 2009: Created SaniShop micro-franchise for economic empowerment of rural folks.
- 2012: His film *Meet Mr Toilet* premiers at the Sundance Film Festival and at the Cannes Lions Festival in 2013.
- 2012: WTO audience reached 3.3 billion.
- 2013: Appointed Adjunct Professor at College of Management Academic Study, teaching Social Entrepreneurship.
- 2013: Singapore government successfully helped WTO by tabling the UN General Assembly to adopt 19 November as the Official UN World Toilet Day.
- 2014: Appointed Adjunct Professor at Taylors University Malaysia.

LEADING YOURSELF

As an introduction, what were some of your leadership milestones? What were some of the leadership transitions that you went through?

As a child, I was very playful and as the youngest in the family, I was always forgiven when I misbehaved. In school, I was considered a failure as I could not enter a university or polytechnic. But that created an opportunity where I had nothing to lose and thus after my first job as a salesman for three years, I ventured into business. To me, it was so much easier to do well in business than in my studies.

I started trading in building materials and found an investor who believed in me because I was a good salesman. Together, we secured a $4 million contract supplying acoustic partitions to the Raffles City Convention Centre in my first year of starting the business, and then started to sell roofing tiles and bricks. Business was so good that we eventually started an acoustic partition joint-venture factory with a German company, a roof tile joint factory with the French, and a brick factory joint-venture with Malaysian and Taiwanese companies. Eventually, we also went into real estate development where we built the Australian International School.

As a salesman, honesty was the main reason my customers were loyal. If my products were not the most suitable for them, I would recommend my competitor's products instead. This made my customers feel that I put their interests first. In business partnerships, I tell people exactly what the deal is and I usually take a minority role so that everybody wins. Because we were always profitable, our investors kept coming back. Consequently, I started 16 businesses, always as a minority shareholder and leveraging on the expertise and resources of other people. I now teach the "Leverage Model" at universities on how to use other people's money, talent, time and align their objectives to yours so that mutually beneficial outcomes can be shared.

> THE IDEA: Leverage your skills and strengths
> with complementary talents from others and you
> will achieve tremendous multiplier impact for
> mutual parties.

What led you to becoming a social entrepreneur/leader?

After I created the 16 businesses, I started to realise that money was no longer an objective. After your stomach is full and you have attained financial independence, the focus should be how to devote the rest of your time to society. A lot of people say that they will focus on their family. That is a given, but you have more capacity than that. For me, my calculation is quite simple. The reason why we have to focus on society is that the real currency of life is time. When you don't have money, you sell time to buy money. But if you have money, selling time to buy money becomes a loss-making business! Thus, you need a higher and more meaningful value in exchange for your time. Even if you don't use your time wisely, you will still spend it, and the search for meaning becomes more urgent as time goes by.

I estimate that I will die when I am 80 years old, so I now have approximately 8,000 days left to live, and I have to do more and more. The philosophy is that between the time I arrived in the world and the time I leave, I have to make a difference. Death is a big motivator for me because I want to be as useful as possible before I die.

> THE IDEA: As macabre as it may sound, thinking
> of "death" forces us to make the best of the life
> we have.

Was that why you founded the World Toilet Organisation?

I grew up with the British bucket system. It was terrifying as a child to see other people's excrement, dysentery blood and intestinal worms. When we moved from our attap huts to our first Housing Development Board flat, the flush toilet system made us feel like wealthy people. When I was 40, then Singapore Prime Minister Goh Chok Tong said that we should measure our graciousness against the cleanliness of our public toilets. So I started the Restroom Association (Singapore) to clean up our public toilets.

After that, I realised there were 15 other toilet associations around the world without headquarters. I offered to form the World Toilet Organisation and we created an instant world body without any money, staff or authority. The media gave me all the legitimacy we needed and eventually the brand became reality when supporters all over the world started speaking out and taking action towards the cause. In 2013, we broke the global taboo when the UN General Assembly adopted our founding day, 19 November, as the UN World Toilet Day. We want to use this legitimacy to work with every country and to ensure that everyone everywhere has access to safe, clean and sustainable toilets.

In your journey as a leader, did you have any role models? Who inspired you to be the leader that you are?

I am very inspired by my grandmother and my mother. My grandmother for her altruism: she had no money, but being an elder in the family, she was able to mobilise funds from relatives who were better off to help the ones in need. She was an iconoclast who didn't care about legal systems or norms. In the early days, she actually smuggled our entire family from Indonesia into Singapore and "converted" them into Singapore residents. To me this was amazing, because if we still lived in the Riau Islands, we would be so poor today. While she actually broke the law to accomplish this, she delivered a lot of talented people into Singapore who have since contributed significantly to the economy. Her act of "lawlessness" reminds me of the 15 people in Philadelphia who committed treason against the British crown to found independent America. Without them doing so, there would be no America today! I think that you always have to be moral and ethical, but you may not always need to be legal. Because to be legal all the time means that you are preserving the status quo and if the status quo is unacceptable, then you have to take the risk. But you have to do it for the greater good, not for yourself.

My second role model is my mother, who taught me the value of social entrepreneurship. In the early days, my father earned very little money as a grocery store assistant and was unable to feed the entire family. My mother, who was not educated, began to conduct business. She would go to the community centre and pay a dollar for a sewing lesson and thereafter organise a class herself to teach six students for a dollar each, thus making a 500% yield of $5! From the sewing skills she learnt, she became a haberdasher, buying cloth and other materials and teaching her students to produce decorative cushions. She then sold these to car owners, making a 20% profit after paying her students. In essence, my mother was doing agency, distribution, salesmanship, branding, promotion, bulk-breaking and social entrepreneurship through this form of job creation for the village women. At a very early age of five, I had already attended business school through the experiences of my mother and grandmother. Of course, I did not realise it until I became an adult. It's amazing how role models shape a child's future.

From my father, I learnt about loyalty. He would never leave the grocery store he was working at even though there was a lot of hardship for very little pay. When I asked him why did he not quit after 35 years of earning a paltry of salary of $350 a month, he said to me, "I have worked 35 years in this shop. If this is not my shop, whose is it?" At that moment, I learnt from him that ownership of decision is the real ownership where the boss lets you make decisions without you owning a share of the shop. That influenced my style of management – here at the World Toilet Organisation, I ask all my employees to self-manage. That is why they are so motivated and approaching every day with energy. I am not their boss, but their facilitator. I don't draw a salary from WTO so every funding that we get pays their salaries and the projects. The employees here have the best of both worlds, knowing that as they do good they receive spiritual reward, and at the same time are able to feed their families and themselves.

With all these role models, do you have some leadership guiding principles that you live by? What is your personal mantra to leading yourself?

I have a very poor memory, so I cannot tell lies. Because to tell a lie, I have to remember it in case somebody were to ask me again and to defend a lie, you need several more lies, and even more again. You need a fantastic memory to be a liar. Thus, to keep a good reputation as a salesperson I always told the customer the truth, which was very rare in our business. I would tell customers when my product did not meet the job requirements and recommend a competitor who had the right product. In doing so, the customer could always trust my recommendations and since I put them first instead of my products, they did not bother to look for other sources and I thus built a very loyal bunch of customers.

The other philosophy is that people like ideas that are appealing and meaningful, but before they can collaborate with you, they must trust and like you first. I am a firm believer of authenticity in all that you do. You have to accept yourself, acknowledege all your weaknesses and strengths, tell people who you are, have an ability to laugh at yourself, to not always be correct, to apologise and to know what you can and cannot do and tell others so without being ashamed.

> THE IDEA: Being transparent In your deeds and words greatly accelerates trust-building and collaborative efforts.

How do you manage your time and energy as leader, since you have so many conflicting projects?

I think energy comes from fun; if something is fun, you will have more energy. Whatever I do, I choose things that are fun, neglected, difficult, new to me, things that others don't want to do – these are things that I enjoy very much.

I am very motivated to achieve a result that can create meaningful social value for everybody. I work harder now than when I was running businesses. Back then, I had time to play golf and have long lunches, but now I have no time – even my nights are dedicated to skype sessions with my counterparts in Europe and America. Typically, this would be very taxing for a person who is forced to do it, but if you are willing to do it, it is not strenuous.

I am very blessed to have a confident wife who has a big support network from her family and friends. She is a real estate agent and is always busy with our four children and also takes care of other family members whenever they are in need. So she is like me, using every second of the day. On weekends, we do steal a few moments to drink a cup of coffee or play mahjong with a regular group of friends. We have been married for 23 years now and are still crazily in love.

Can you think of a time when you didn't succeed the way you wanted to, and how did you bounce back from that failure?

There were several instances. I was 24 years old in the first year that I started the acoustic partition business, and tendered a price that was a million dollars lower than what would be an appropriate tender price for the Raffles City project. I was awarded the contract as a result, which meant that I had to fulfil the contract at a substantial loss. It took a week for me to figure out how to work out the issue. I went back to the Raffles City management and told them that I made a mistake and could not execute the contract. I told them that they could punish me in any way that they thought fit. Miraculously, they told me to name the new price and I replied that I needed $1.1 million more. After a quick discussion among themselves, they agreed to the new price. They respected an honest businessman with a quality product. That was a week of sleepless nights, but I emerged from the incident a wiser person. Eventually, we successfully continued the contract and I managed to keep the trust between myself and my client intact.

What was the second experience?

The second time was in 1997 during the currency crisis. I owned 10% of the building material company while my brother owned 5% and we employed about 45 employees. Business was really difficult at the time because orders were not coming in and staff were resigning. While we still managed to break even, the remaining partners wanted to sell their shares because they did not believe that the market would recover. Real estate prices were falling. Not wanting to affect our employees, my brother and I had to double mortgage our houses to buy out the remaining 85% of shares.

I had the energy to execute this turnaround because I did something quite strange. In the midst of my crisis, I created the World Toilet Organisation, on top of the Restroom Association that I had already started. My staff and partners were astonished that I still had time to do something else for fun despite the distress. I told them that if I were to stay in the office all day, I would go crazy because there was no good news in the company with everything falling apart. During that time, I was in the office only till lunch time, and spent my remaining time at the WTO. The fun I had outside of work allowed me to retain my sanity and derive creative solutions to do a turnaround management. It was a very stressful period during which we had to turn every piece of inventory into cash and we even discounted debts to ensure that there was cash flow. We were able to make a lot of compromises to ensure that the company weathered the recession period, keeping the company afloat and retaining all the employees who wanted to stay. I was quite exhausted by the end of 2005 and informed the general manager to completely take over the business. I did not want to wait for another recession to distract me from dedicating all of my time to social work.

> THE IDEA: **Finding a source of energy booster outside of work can bring in new ideas and passion into the daily grind of routine.**

LEADING OTHERS

In your opinion, what makes a good leader?

When I was a salesman in Diethelm (now Diethelm Keller), I could not make the manager grade because I did not have a university degree. Instead, I became a Union Secretary at the Singapore Manual & Mercantile Workers' Union and realised that true leadership is not about hierarchical power but servanthood. If you empower people and make them the boss and hold them accountable, it makes leading so much easier. Instead of leading them, you help them to lead. You make leaders out of people.

A good leader needs to mobilise their people to be enthusiastic and to take ownership and groom them to be leaders. It takes humility and self confidence to allow others to be greater than you. If you care about accomplishing or progressing the mission, then you will want to mobilise a lot of leaders to make it happen. The mission is paramount and you are the servant to the mission. A shared vision is very similar to creating shared values. That is the type of leadership that I try to practice everyday.

> THE IDEA: A good leader is ultimately a good servant who aims to meet the needs of his/her followers before their own

What makes you a good leader then?

When I founded the World Toilet Organisation, I knew that if you want to be a leader, you threaten the egos of others. But if you want to be a servant, everybody will love you.

Finding neglected agendas such as toilet sanitation or poverty alleviation and being able to make a fool of myself to experiment with solutions to these makes me a servant-leader. The world is full of followers who are highly intelligent and capable, but they have high safety needs. My servant leadership approach makes these people leaders and builds their self esteem. At the end of the day, it does not matter what title they use to refer to you, but whether you can mobilise others to successfully complete the mission that you all set out to achieve. It's an adaptive process and others will be motivated if you are there to make them shine and not to claim the credit for their work.

> THE IDEA: Rather than chasing the latest fad or "hot" topic, the astute leader searches out for the neglected agenda or upcoming trend to champion

Should you always adopt one style of leadership?

Different situations require different types of leadership. For example, without Mr Lee Kuan Yew's strong hand in the early days of Singapore's independence, he may not have been able to guide Singapore. When starting out, one may sometimes need to adopt a benevolent dictatorship style, but as things progress, you will need to switch to a consultative leadership style. In today's day and age of the Internet, increasingly educated people and wide availability of information, you will need to be an adaptive leader according to what the situation requires of you. You need to have empathy for people and bring out the best in them.

What is your philosophy with regard to attracting talent, and how do you retain them to continue working for this cause?

Tell people what you are doing and have a clear vision, and suitable people will naturally come forth. I give a lot of talks in different circles and I think this rubs off in many quarters. If you are honest and transparent, crooks tend to not like you. Crooks like ostentatious, egoistic people whom they can trick and later exploit. But when you don't present them with the opportunity, they will avoid you and it helps you to weed them out.

I practise distribution of ownership by making others leaders. In doing so, I don't have to do that much work and it frees up a lot of creative space for me to innovate. I'm not very good at fundraising and sometimes I lose talented people when I run out of money. It makes me very sad but I'm still learning how to fundraise so I can avoid such regrets.

What is your philosophy on leveraging others for success?

I'm not good at fundraising but I'm good at "friends raising" and they often support my work in kind instead of money. The leverage model requires that the partners who are being leveraged upon gain more than you. If you are a leverage-social entrepreneur, you give each of your partner much more than you gain in that bilateral deal. However, because you are leveraging a lot of people, you are a multi-lateral entrepreneur, so you ultimately get a lot more benefit than the single bilateral deals. In the end, the mission benefits. If you want a good leverage model, you have to subject yourself to the mission and not become the mission.

When I first appeared in the media, I was very happy and enjoyed the attention, which was intoxicating. After a while, I felt that I had fallen into an ego trap and asked myself what was going on. Eventually, I took a step back and concluded that my enjoyment of the media visibility was a natural process. However, I had to remember that all of it was for the mission and that I was merely a tool towards inspiring others to the cause.

> THE IDEA: Leaders are constantly under the spotlight but must use the attention to focus on the mission rather than themselves.

What was one leadership challenge that was memorable for you?

In the 16 businesses that I manage, I am able to pay for very good quality management people because we are in the commercial business. In the social sector, it is quite difficult from a human resource point of view to assemble a group of highly energised people. In the NGO sector, you will find that even if a person has been working there for 10 years, it doesn't mean that he or she has 10 years of quality experience. That was one of the biggest challenges that slowed down the process. It's difficult to find talent in the commercial sector, but it's even more difficult to find talent in the social sector.

I have also created the BOP Hub, a non-profit venture that aims to provide a global platform to forge strategic partnerships between the private sector, social enterprises and subject matter experts with the aim of ending poverty by creating a vibrant marketplace for the base of the social pyramid. The dreams are ambitious and you need people with big brains and big hearts. But I remain optimistic so I can be energised and carry on.

LEADING THE ORGANISATION

What are your current challenges in leading the World Toilet Organisation and the BOP Hub?

The dream is ambitious and the capacity to fulfil the dream is still in the developmental stage. So the challenge is how to use very few people to leverage a large number of people externally. For example, partnership and strategic alliance can bring about mutual joy and benefit. This allows us to achieve a bigger impact without scaling up our organisation. The challenge is to be a highly intelligent connective coordinator and not just a matchmaker. Each resource comes with its vested interest and we need to align various interests to achieve an exponential impact without us paying a single dollar.

This has been the magic behind the World Toilet Organisation for the past 17 years and this will be the magic of the BOP Hub. The Hub allows us to think without limitations, and everyone will gravitate towards a good idea as long as you are able to articulate clearly how it fits with their organisational philosophy and mission. This alignment will create great synergy that can reduce wastage. You have to believe that people will come forward to work with you. It's not egoism, it's optimism.

What is your vision for the World Toilet Organisation and the BOP Hub?

My vision for the World Toilet Organisation is that clean toilets and proper sanitation will become a norm throughout the world. That everyone will have access to a clean, safe toilet anytime they need it. If we successfully promote market-based solutions, we will solve the problem within 15 to 20 years. Today, 40% of the population does not have access to a toilet, that's approximately 2.5 billion people. But I believe this can solved if people see toilets as a must-have, a status symbol and an object of desire. After driving demand, we need to drive supply by training the poor to produce toilets and sell them locally with a profit. The SaniShop micro-franchise creates jobs and is very sustainable after we train the locals. With the Internet and globalisation, solutions can be replicated very quickly. We are partnering many companies to move this model. Our pride and joy is that every time we have an idea, others can use it as their own and even improve on these ideas to become more efficient. We can't do it by ourselves. No one person is bigger than all of us combined.

The mission of the BOP Hub is to make all seven billion people in the world part of our formal economy. Currently, only three billion are in our formal economy, while the other four billion (who form the base of the social pyramid) are excluded. I believe that businesses are increasingly excited to serve the poor as their customers and we want to accelerate this to the extent that there will be no more NGOs and social entrepreneurs in the world, but only socially-conscious companies who will compete to serve the poor so that they have access to quality of life, jobs, entrepreneurship to become part of the supply chain and to have higher spending power. When that happens, there will only be one problem to solve – how to avoid 4 billion new polluters on the planet. It will be about finding a median point where the poor and the rich consume resources in a sustainable manner. This solution has not yet arrived, but we will have to prevent it now and we may have to change the way the world measures wealth and success.

Perhaps in the future, a millionaire will be someone who has improved the lives of a million people, and not merely one who has a million dollars.

What is your final advice for social entrepreneurs or people who wish to start an NGO or a social enterprise? What are some things to be mindful of?

It will be good for new social entrepreneurs to intern with more established ones, because there is currently so much drive to create start-ups without recognising that there are already established organisations that can help to mentor them and create synergies. In my opinion, most of the young social enterprises fail because the fuel that drives them to set up these organisations is more ego-centric than altruism. My advice for young social entrepreneurs is: if you are angry about something, think of and offer a solution, have a constructive conversation with someone who might be helpful towards deriving that answer. Don't stop at being angry with a social problem. Convert your anger into constructive motivation to take on such responsibilities and start to create a responsible and pro-active culture to create a fairer world.

> THE IDEA: It is a human condition to complain about what's wrong with the world but the leader stands out to make it "right".

BERNARD TAN KOK KIANG
President, Commercial Business Group
Singapore Technologies Kinetics Ltd

INCULCATE A STRATEGIC VISION TO DRIVE CHANGE

BERNARD TAN KOK KIANG was appointed president of the Commercial Business Group, Singapore Technologies Kinetics Ltd (ST Kinetics), in March 2014. ST Kinetics is the land systems and specialty vehicles arm of Singapore Technologies Engineering Ltd (ST Engineering), a company listed on the Singapore Exchange.

He leads the Commercial Business Group (CBG), one of ST Kinetics' two key pillars, and is responsible for growing the Group's Specialty Vehicles, Services and Technology businesses.

Before joining ST Kinetics, Bernard led a career in the military and government, holding a variety of leadership positions, before making a successful transition into the financial sector. In 2008, he joined DBS Bank as Managing Director in Debt Capital Market, Global Financial Markets. He proceeded to lead DBS's acquisition of Bowa Bank in Taiwan, and head DBS Bank's regional operations as Acting Country Head of DBS Taiwan and President Commissioner of PT Bank DBS Indonesia respectively.

Bernard won two of Singapore's prestigious scholarships, the President's Scholarship and the Lee Kuan Yew Postgraduate Scholarship. He graduated from the University of Birmingham, UK with first class honours in Economics and Political Science and from the Massachusetts Institute of Technology, USA with a Masters in Business Administration.

Bernard has been a Board Member of Sports SG since 2006, and was appointed Vice President of the Football Association of Singapore in October 2013. He is an active sportsman and a regular runner and golfer, as well as plays social soccer.

His other appointments include being a president commissioner of Anglomas International Bank in Indonesia, a director of Premier Corporation in Singapore and the chairman of the Singapore Chamber of Commerce in Indonesia.

Bernard has lived abroad for extended periods in the UK, US, Taiwan and Indonesia, and speaks three languages, namely English, Chinese and Bahasa Indonesia.

He is married with three children.

LEADING YOURSELF

How did you start from when you graduated to where you are now?

I joined the Singapore Armed Forces (SAF) straight out of junior college and went through the basic training. I went to university to study and returned as a combat officer in the Armour division. Over the next 18 years, I was fortunate to hold a series of command and staff appointments and rose to the rank of Brigadier General at the age of 36. My last appointment was Director of Military Intelligence (DMI). I was the last Director of Joint Intelligence Directorate (DIID) before the appointment was renamed. I left the SAF after holding the appointment for two-and-half years. When I left, I serendipitously joined DBS bank. I was first in Debt Capital Markets for a very short while, before leading the acquisition of a bank in Taiwan. I did this for a year. After that, I joined DBS Indonesia and headed the franchise there as the Country Head for the next four years. My last year with DBS was again spent heading an acquisition team. Just early this year, I joined ST Kinetics as the president of the Commercial Business Group in ST Kinetics and have been there for five months to date.

What is your perspective of leadership? What does it mean to you?

Leaders have a compelling vision that people will follow. Ultimately, the definition of leadership is to incite change and this requires a strong drive. If you do not incite change, I don't think that really constitutes leadership. Unless leaders constantly induce change in an organisation, it's basically just management.

You do have to learn these traits, and I was very fortunate to have been in the SAF where leadership is always emphasised.

More importantly, you are thrown into positions of leadership – sometimes even when you are not fully ready. The philosophy of the SAF is to allow leaders to grow into the role and many progressive organisations do the same to groom its leaders. I was also developed as a generalist and thrown into many different professions and constantly trying to develop breadth, perhaps at the expense of depth. But breadth is very important when you are running a very large organisation. I owe this very much to the SAF.

> THE IDEA: Never stagnate in your leadership quest and with time and experience, by reflecting on your actions and those of others, you deepen the understanding of yourself and what it means to be a leader.

Who were some of your leadership role models and what lessons did you learn from them?

Along the way, three leaders stood out for me. One was a senior civil servant. When I was a young officer, he was already very influential, but his style of leading was very quiet, almost a cerebral style of leading in which the conversation was done very quietly but, at the same time, extremely insightful. That struck me as one way of influencing people – explaining in a quiet and patient way why we do certain things. He also broke a lot of the hierarchy because he would come down to speak to you at your level. I was a captain then and there were, of course, many levels in between us. But he would sometimes come down and have a conversation with me, and I would always feel that I walked away wiser. I've always held that as a benchmark of how I influence other people – do people become wiser from the conversations they have with me?

> THE IDEA: You do not need to be an extrovert to
> lead – leadership is a big word but it boils down
> to having meaningful conversations with someone
> and helping them believe that they can be a better
> version of themselves.

Who was the second leader who inspired you?

The next one was a CEO of a public listed company but his interaction with me was as the chairman of a statutory board. His style of leading was not too different from the first – he was also a quiet leader, not boisterous, but he would engage you. With him, you felt that he was interested in you as a person. This CEO would take the time to talk to you individually, explain to you what his issues were, and tried to extract from you your issues and insights. During meetings, he would ensure that you contributed by going to you and saying, "Bernard, what do you think?" That method of leadership forced you to do two things. First, he encouraged you to form an opinion, which is important for a leader. Second, he quickly made you feel part of the team, which to me was quite extraordinary. Surprisingly, not many chairmen of meetings do this. I continue to meet him and regard him as one of my mentors in life. I remembered him telling me that if there was one thing that leaders don't do enough of, it's thinking. When we go into the office, we start clearing the emails. Halfway through, the secretary knocks on your door and before you know it, meeting number one takes place, and then meeting number two, meeting number three, meeting number four, and off you go and the day is done. Tomorrow, you'll repeat the same thing – but when do you actually have quiet time to think?

> THE IDEA: We can be caught up with meetings and neglect the importance of thinking. Leaders are prized for their insight and opinions – the more you think, the better your insights.

What did he inspire you in terms of thinking?

Thinking alone is important. If you are an extrovert, you may argue that you think in a group and you bounce ideas off people. That's where you get energy from. But you still need to prepare. Before you go for a meeting, ask what it is that you really want to get out of that meeting. What impact do you want to have on the people in the meeting? What impact do you want to get from them in the meeting? When you meet a client, are you clear what your objectives for the client are? Most importantly, you have to link all your activities back to the outcomes you seek to achieve. Ask yourself if the things that you're doing this week will contribute to your goals this week, this month or this year? If you're not organising your day moving towards your longer term objectives, are you really spending your time correctly? Leaders who are very busy get caught up with day-to-day activities that they forget to ask if they are doing the right things steering the organisation towards the longer term goal. To me, this was tremendously impactful as a learning point.

> THE IDEA: Link your short-term actions to long-term goals, ask yourself – will the things that I'm going to do this week contribute to my longer term goal that I want to achieve in a week, in a month or in a year?

And the final role model?

The third role model was when I was in the banking industry. One of my seniors had a huge capacity and energy to understand the business right down to the smallest details. Whether this comes from his years in banking or his personality – I'm more inclined to think that it's his personality – it is an incredible way of leading a business. Sometimes you think that leading businesses only requires a strategic vision while leaving the details of execution to other people. This CEO showed me that both are interlinked. Unless you have a feel for the details, it is incredibly difficult for you to know how to pull levers to reach a certain goal. Management by objectives is not correct until you understand the specifics.

> THE IDEA: Do not focus purely on strategic outcomes and ignore the link to details of operations on the ground.

Can you be trained to be a leader?

I believe people have an innate bias for leadership, but nurturing and development is very important. Is there a way to train leaders? I think there are principles but the best training is if you put leaders under good leaders.

Having learnt from all these role models, what are three things that define you as a leader?

Leaders must have a strong drive to incite change. In order to do so, you need to have a strategic vision. It is surprising, but if you ask a lot of people in many organisations what they envision their organisation to be like in five years, the answer is mostly what it is like today. Leaders need to inculcate a strategic vision to drive change.

How do you formulate one? I think it is difficult to formulate this strategic vision in isolation – you need to take input from others. It is rumoured that our late Minister Mentor Mr Lee Kuan Yew was voracious in gathering information from multiple conversations with a wide variety of people – he would talk to professors, scientists and reporters. His view of the world was basically formulated by an amalgamation of everything, and he tested his biases with people. It is the same in business. You need to understand your competitors, your customers, evolving technology, new regulations and other market dynamics. Only then can you form a view of the changes needed. Because of this, I believe that a leader in a new organisation requires about six months to sense-make.

THE IDEA: A good leader needs to have broad access to information of present and future scenarios in order to sense-make before starting to implement bold changes.

What is the second quality?

The second is the ability to align everyone in the organisation with a common goal and vision. Sometimes organisational hurdles prevent alignment from taking place, sometimes it is structural. But usually it just involves getting everybody to row in the same direction. This involves plenty of communication – not just downwards, but laterally as well as upward. In my last job, I watched the CEO build alignment between management and the board. There were also repeated conversations downwards throughout the organisation. This communication kept all of us on the same path. Communication is the key to alignment.

> THE IDEA: If you fail to align everyone towards a common vision and goal you will not get traction in your change agenda. Communication is key.

And the final one?

The last one is execution. This revolves around having good people on your team. My last boss told me that all managers overestimate their ability to influence and coach subordinates. It is difficult to improve "C" performers to "B" performers, let alone if you want "A" results, which would require a team of "A" and "B" people. Sometimes we persist with a team of "C"s because we think we can make them "A"s. I have learnt that this is wrong. The football analogy is apt – if you have a team struggling to avoid relegation and you want the team to compete, you need to bring in good players. By all means, develop the youth team, but your current players need to deliver, and if that means bringing in better players, so be it.

> THE IDEA: Having a strong team and making sure they are "A" players not only frees up your time to coach and train but also will activate the performance of younger players down the line.

What gets you out of bed every day?

I enjoy work, I enjoy the challenges in my work. I think if you don't enjoy your work, you are probably in the wrong job. There is satisfaction in making an organisation a far better place than it was previously. There is pressure for results in a very short time frame. People do want to see results in a short time, although substantial change takes at least years.

I've asked myself when I was most energised in my career. My best working experience was in a place where a group of us felt that we were unconstrained to change the way we did business. Basically, we could do anything and because of the group, we knew our ideas would be listened to. The team members were also genuinely collaborative. We were a close-knit group and were friends. We are still friends today.

I have no doubt that I do my best work in a collaborative environment. But leadership is situational. You cannot take one standard mode of leadership and hope for it to succeed everywhere.

As a leader, what is your philosophy of managing your own calendar and time?

We need to guard our calendars jealously and be very careful what we say yes too. We need to say "no" more often to free up time to think and learn. I reckon that most people spend less than 5% of their time thinking, but thinking is the most important activity. Half your time should be spent outside the office, meeting people, developing leads and understanding developments – in short, sensemaking.

> THE IDEA: Be jealous of your time and be wary of others who "steal" your time without clearly stating what the value of your contribution will be.

How do you make decisions at work?

There are a few ways we do decision-making. One way is to decide as a committee – all of us make decisions regarding everything – this is the most inefficient way to run an organisation but the most collegial. My feel is that organisations are now too large for everyone to participate on every issue.

In larger organisations, you therefore need two kinds of meetings. The first is a decision-making meeting which can be smaller and issue dependent while the second is an information-dissemination meeting involving everyone. This can be done once a month or fortnightly just to make sure that everyone is on the same page. Having two kinds of meetings frees up time.

> THE IDEA: Distinguish between information-dissemination meetings versus decision-making ones and whom to invite to which accordingly.

LEADING OTHERS

What makes someone a good leader?

Having good strategic vision, tremendous communication skills, attention to detail, being a talent attractor and a motivator. To get the maximum out of most people, you need to be a motivator. To motivate senior leaders, you need to give them autonomy. The idea of autonomy is a difficult one. If you give autonomy to a novice, the results are going to be disastrous. Before you give someone autonomy, you need to check if he or she is able to deliver. Leaders need to make this assessment. The provision of autonomy with the expectation that people will automatically give great results is simply not true. It is also risky, especially in industries where there is a huge backlash on regulatory issues such as banking, or on the environment like in oil and gas industries. Building trust requires time and repeated interaction. Getting comfortable with people requires a particular mindset. People respond to bosses who are fair, who set clear objectives instead of fuzzy ones, to someone who comes up and gives you a pat on your back and says well done from time to time, and who speaks clearly when he is unhappy about something.

> THE IDEA: Empowerment and autonomy are great
> motivational tools signalling trust given to the
> employee, but the trust needs to be developed
> and tested over the initial few months of working
> together.

What makes leaders fail?

The first reason is "what worked before will work in the future" – the failure to have foresight. Many people are very comfortable doing what they did before. A leader is always looking for change, and therefore he is very open to what he can do better and open to the fact that what may have been right in the past may not be right tomorrow. A leader needs to be a learner.

I think a multitude of issues can impede a leader's ability to learn. Success is a drug that can induce complacency and over-confidence such that a leader becomes lazy. A leader may also be so far removed from the world that their ability to make sense of things disappears – immediate subordinates filter out bad news and only offer the good. This is why as a leader, you have to keep open channels. You must cut ranks and talk to people at all levels. You must have conversations with people who will give you honest answers and tell you the unpleasant news. This is easier said than done as good news always travels faster than bad news.

There is also the issue of not being able to execute people management decisions. Sometime we persist with a team that is simply not capable enough. I know it is difficult to fire people. I like to form relationships with the people I work with, and once you do that, it is very hard to make the call. But I've learnt in the past that performance is very much related to the team you have on your bench, so one must make the difficult decisions.

Lastly, it is a lack of communication. You may have a good team and you may have a good strategy, but you are not communicating it upwards, downwards and sideways. You don't get alignment within the team and no one understands the eventual goal and vision.

> THE IDEA: **It is dangerous for leaders to cocoon themselves away from others or to only surround themselves with followers whom they trust.**

Share an example of you taking on a leadership challenge that showcased you at your best.

I think the best leadership experience was the takeover of a bank in Taiwan in 2008. The mandate was quite simple – we had a hundred days to go in, take over the bank and open operations the day after. In short, this was an intense operation. This was a bank with a balance sheet of over S$8 billion with 40 branches across Taiwan. I led a multinational team of Singaporeans, Taiwanese and Hong Kongers. There were 100 people involved in the entire programme and I answered to the Chief Financial Officer. This integration was described as one of the smoothest ever. I think we did a couple of things right.

First, I had a great team that was motivated and knew what needed to be done, with great leaders who were extremely clear and detailed. Second, we communicated well. We met three times a week to make sure everyone was on the same page. Communication wasn't just among the integration team, but with all members in the bank. We spent a tremendous amount of time talking. In short, we over communicated to every one, conducting road shows across the island. We wanted the staff of the local bank to feel as though they were joining a much larger family rather than feeling that they were being gobbled up. It helped that a lot of us were able to speak mandarin, and it helped that we got on very well as a team. We lived in the same hotel for four months, which produced a college dorm atmosphere. The core integration team became very close friends. If you ask people still working in DBS who were involved in the Bowa project, I would wager that they would say that this was one of the best projects they've ever worked on. I was just fortunate to be in that position to lead them.

What are the leadership lessons that you've learnt?

My worst leadership moment was to try and emulate a very stern and authoritarian leader. This completely didn't work for me and it negatively affected my relationship with the people around me. I still have regrets but I've now put it past me and cast it as a learning event when I was young .

My second bad leadership moment involved being lax with performance management. I persisted with a team that really couldn't make the grade. I couldn't make the hard decisions, but that was again a learning experience. Moving on, I've more or less come to terms with the fact that stellar performance requires some hard decisions.

> THE IDEA: Leadership requires hard decisions and you have to let your people go at times when the fit or their motivation does not fit the requirement for new roles. Do it quickly and respectfully and the affected may even thank you for it.

LEADING THE ORGANISATION

You've moved from a very straight bureaucratic government organisation to a multi-national bank to ST Kinetics. What does it take for someone to move with such agility within various industries?

A sense of adventure? In the military, the systems are very good, and values are very important. The people that you work with are truly excellent. The friends you make are extraordinary – being in a uniform service, you crawl through mud together and the camaraderie that is formed from sharing tough times with each other cannot be replicated anywhere else. There is a strong sense of mission.

A commercial organisation is a very different animal. While there are similar traits, the focus is on the bottom line. In government, there is no equivalent bottom line. In the commercial world, this requires ensuring that your customers are happy. I have found that there is an adrenaline rush in chasing the bottom line. When I put my hand up for any job, I now prefer a profit and loss (P&L) job.

What advice would you give to a young leader in terms of coping with office politics?

I think cut-throat office politics are unhealthy and should not exist in any organisation. Decisions should not be personality-based and promotions should be based on merit. Any company that does otherwise is a bad company. A company also needs to have an open culture where you can say anything so long as you keep professional respect for each other, and not just say what the boss wants to hear. If an organisation is overly political, I think you should get out of it. If you are working in an organisation where you feel that you and your supervisor don't get along, you should get out if you feel the situation cannot be salvaged. You can only do your best if your boss believes in you.

> THE IDEA: Do not make people decisions simply based on your judgement of how certain individuals' personalities and traits appeal to you. This creates unnecessary cronyism and office politics.

Tell me a bit about the organisation that you're currently leading, and the top challenges that you face.

ST Kinetics has an annual turnover of between $1.5 to $1.6 billion. I think the key challenge is to keep up with change. For technology companies, the pace of change is very fast. We need to keep the right pace. The real challenge is making sure that the bets for the future do come through.

What are you currently doing to cope with this?

I go through the same process. The first is to sense-make, and then form a strategy and vision. It takes some time, perhaps six months. Subsequently, we have to make sure that we have that alignment and ability to execute the strategy within the company to drive towards those areas of change. I am excited because we are laying a new foundation. There are good things that have been done in the past and there are huge advantages that a company our size has in navigating the change.

There is a lot of focus now on the influx of foreign workers coming into organisations who are a lot more ambitious than our local leaders. What's your take on how leaders can step up?

I think Singaporeans are good in terms of many things, but not so good in others. We can do better in being global citizens. Singaporeans don't like to venture abroad. Somehow we have grown very comfortable in Singapore. I think the reasons for this could be multifarious. Some suggest that life in Singapore is simply too comfortable. Others suggest that our education system restricts family mobility. I think working abroad is crucial to the development of an international leader. We simply need more people to go abroad.

The second area is in the area of creativity – the realm of solving undefined problems. We are very good at solving problems that are defined – if there's an equation, we can solve it. But if you ask what the equation should be, that's more challenging. I think the solving of defined problems has served us extremely well in the first and second lap in Singapore's history. In the third lap now, we need to think outside the box and solve undefined problems. This requires systems thinking.

Thirdly, we probably need to communicate better. Many people from other nations are great communicators. We tend to be less polished. To be good leaders, we have to be able to influence not just our own people but everyone else. We don't do this well enough.

> THE IDEA: To groom new generation leaders, focus on internationalisation opportunities, creative thinking and communication competencies.

What's your final word of advice for a young engineer who has just started work at ST Kinetics?

The first thing is to be a good engineer. Developing a solid foundation and a good skill base is always important in any career. Go abroad, gain foreign experience. In later life, the question will emerge: do you want to be a specialist or a generalist? If you want to be a specialist, you need to be very good in your chosen field. If you want to be a generalist, you have to broaden your skillset. Add on other leadership skills – communication, lateral thinking, strategising, broaden your view of the industry. Do not confine your definition of learning to what you are doing today, but to anything you can pick up along the way.

One important thing: be yourself. There are other people whose leadership styles are very effective and you would like to be like them. But this may not be you. Be comfortable in your own skin.

THE IDEA: In your early years as a leader, focus on deepening your skillsets, and later, on broadening your experience with lateral moves or international experiences. Always hunger to learn from new assignments and people whom you interact with. Finally, be comfortable with who you are and be the best version of yourself!

TAN CHUAN JIN
Minister of Manpower
Minister for Social and Family Development.

BUILD TRUST AS A LEADER

TAN CHUAN JIN served in the Singapore Armed Forces (SAF) for nearly 24 years before retiring in 2011. Commissioned at Sandhurst, he has held various appointments in the SAF, including Commander Singapore 3rd Division and Commander Training and Doctrine Command.

When the Indian Ocean Tsunami struck on Boxing Day 2004, Mr Tan led the SAF's relief effort to Meulaboh, Aceh in Indonesia. Despite the uncertainty and scale of the crisis, they brought in emergency relief to stabilise the situation in the critical period after the tragedy.

As chairman of the executive committee, Mr Tan was responsible for organising the National Day Parade in 2009.

In May 2011, Mr Tan was elected as one of the Members of Parliament for the Marine Parade Group Representation

Constituency. He was then appointed as Minister of State for National Development and Manpower.

On 1 August 2012, Mr Tan was appointed Acting Minister for Manpower, and concurrently Senior Minister of State for National Development. Mr Tan relinquished his National Development portfolio on 1 September 2013, but continued to helm the Ministry of Manpower as Acting Minister. He was made a full minister on 1 May 2014. On 9 April 2015, Mr Tan was appointed Minister for Social and Family Development.

Mr Tan was awarded the SAF Overseas Scholarship to read Economics and graduated with a BSc (Econs) from the London School of Economics (1992). He also holds a Masters of Arts in Defence Studies from King's College London (1999), and a Masters in Public Management from the Lee Kuan Yew School of Public Policy, National University of Singapore (2008).

Born in 1969, Mr Tan is married with two children. He is an avid photographer and enjoys reading, watching movies and football.

LEADING YOURSELF

What are your key transition points during your leadership journey?

My leadership journey started in school where I held leadership appointments. However, at the time, it wasn't a deliberate decision to become a leader. Instead, it was the keen sense of wanting to serve. This interest in public service then prompted me to join the SAF. From there, I held different appointments before crossing over to politics. It was my experience with the SAF that eventually shaped my beliefs and approaches to leadership, which then carried over to politics. While the policies may be different with the SAF as compared to my current role as Minister and MP, the approach is pretty much the same.

> THE IDEA: A leader's motive should not be to boss others around but from the premise of wanting to serve others.

Who were your leadership role models and what have you learnt from them?

I do not have a particular role model; rather, I am shaped by the people I have served with. My leadership philosophy comes from observing the people around me, and learning from the positive or negative experiences of others. From there, I am able to sense-make and distill lessons I have learnt into my own leadership philosophy.

Do you have any guidelines or compass points in terms of leading yourself?

It all starts with "self". I believe that a leader must be aware of his or her personal values and beliefs. From there, the leader should think about how to apply these values or beliefs in his or her area of leadership, which for me is the area of public service. I have always believed that leadership, at the most elementary level, is about trust – and trust is about you as a person and whether your followers are able to trust you as their leader, even in times where they may disagree with you. That trust then depends on who you are as a person, and what your values and beliefs are. These may be shaped by your upbringing, individual values and even faith. These values should be articulated with action, since people see you through your actions rather than words.

THE IDEA: Leadership, at the most elementary level, is about trust. While they may disagree with your actions, your followers would always trust the intentions and integrity of a true leader.

How would you describe your leadership philosophy?

A fundamental part of your leadership framework is your values. So you have figure out and be clear about what is it that you believe in. One thing that gets in the way is personal ambition, which is an issue of whether you care for the interest of the organisation or for yourself. When something goes wrong, would you stick your neck out to protect your people? When you do things, are you doing them in order to score points or do you really believe that whatever you are doing is truly important? Your values are important because they shape the way you are as a person and people see that in the way you do things. It is not about what you say, but what you do, which stems from their sense of how authentic you are and what defines you as a person.

For me, integrity is important. It is a fundamental value in order for people to trust you. Another is about caring for others. Do you do something because you genuinely care and are you willing to go that extra mile to make a difference? To me, that is important.

THE IDEA: Decide if your leadership actions are driven by personal ambition or for the genuine interest of the organisation and people involved. People can often see through ulterior motives and it would thus dilute your efforts.

Aside from values, what other attributes are important?

To be a good leader, one also needs to understand what it is that allows you to connect with others. I think the key word here is "engagement". I think people generally want to feel that they can make a difference. How then do you help individuals feel that they are valued and respected? How do you unlock potential in people? We tend to focus on competencies and send people for courses, which develops them in terms of knowledge. However, more time should be spent on developing the individual as a person and as leaders. If people are key to an organisation, then leaders are likewise important, since they are the conduits to enable things to be done. Hence, more should be done to unlock the potential of leaders who are passionate to lead.

> THE IDEA: Leadership development helps to train skillsets but it also develops "heart-sets" and builds character.

How do you manage your time and energy? Could you give me a few examples of how you manage to keep yourself energetic?

Firstly, the nature of my job sustains me. I enjoy my work as an MP a lot, and I believe that I can make a difference. For example, I am always thinking about how I can help lower income families break out of the poverty cycle. Being able to help, even in the smallest ways, through the programmes I run keeps me going.

Secondly, I multi-task to avoid wasting time. However, sometimes, I do feel that sleep is almost a burden. I really need to be sleeping enough, which is something my daughter reminds me to do. So this is something I need to sort out, since I am not getting younger and need the physical rest to sustain myself. Sleep is important because negativity sets in especially when you are very tired.

Thirdly, my family sustains me. While work is important, I prioritise and make time for my family because at the end of the day, no one is indispensable. The country is not going to collapse because you are not there. Family, on the other hand, is all you have and you are all they have. So work-life balance is something I emphasise with the people that work for me. To achieve this, you need to have a clarity of purpose when you are doing something. When that purpose is clearly communicated to the individuals executing it, it avoids second-guessing which ensures that only the necessary is done. This alleviates uncertainty and saves time, which can be better spent on things that are more important, such as family.

> THE IDEA: A leader must first be self-sustaining before taking care of others. Have a solid sleep routine to sustain yourself; catching up on sleep on weekends is a myth.

LEADING OTHERS

Tell me about a particularly challenging moment where you had to rise as a leader.

A key leadership challenge I faced relates to the changing of the Best Unit Competition (BUC) system when I was a Commanding Officer with SAF. The BUC recognises the performance of each Unit by taking into account various performances such as Individual Physical Proficiency Test (IPPT). The previous system was scored in such a way that even if 99% of the unit performs well, the 1%

that does not could affect the score of the entire unit. That was a good system if you wanted to shape competitive behaviour, but it might not be good for morale if your unit came in last. On top of that, there were other equally important objectives to accomplish aside from the BUC, such as live firing. During my time, we did a lot of firing because I believed in its purpose: if we were to go to war, I wanted to make sure that my guys were ready to serve the mission. So I changed the BUC system to a banding process, so if you achieve 90%, it is considered good. While you may be last amongst the unit, it is still possible to be recognised as having attained a good level of performance. That is one example of pushing against a system, and the great thing is that the system allowed you to mobilise the policy and force a change, in spite of being told otherwise.

How about an example when you held office?

The other one would be the entire National Day Parade process in 2009 when I was the chairman of the executive committee. There were several challenges. One of them was to give people behind the scenes due recognition for their contribution. So we thought of ways to increase that exposure, by arranging for the contingent to march through the city from the floating platform to the Padang. In doing so, we were able to engage with the people gathered around who were hoping to see the fireworks. Another example of engagement was through the use of social media, which wasn't a very popular medium among government organisations. By using Facebook, we were able to upload videos showing people and the crew who were behind the scenes during that process, which went viral. Through that, we were able to create recognition for the contributors, which they couyld share with their friends. This experience was very meaningful to be able to help our citizens be a part of nation building.

> THE IDEA: Look for ways to recognise unsung
> heroes that facilitate the outward success of your
> organisation.

LEADING THE ORGANISATION

What is your vision for Singapore's manpower ministry?

It begins with the ministry looking after the people and workers, both Singaporeans and foreigners. While happiness is a concept that is decided by individuals, the ministry should try to provide a climate for people to achieve their aspirations. We have to create a climate for good jobs and opportunities for people to choose from. Next, we have to equip our people and workers to do their jobs. The ministry will continue to work with the Ministry of Education on the education process, the Continued Training (CT) process and vocational training, to equip people with the necessary knowledge and skills. Thirdly, we have to use the information we have to match and allocate people to the available jobs.

There is a lot of focus on grooming Singaporeans to be leaders in MNCs, although there seems to be a glass ceiling where they are great middle-level managers but can't take on C-suite roles. From your perspective, what steps can we take to groom local talent to take on a much more visible C-suite space, in organisations and even global platforms?

I think we have a strong base with education, which is getting stronger. I look at what my kids are doing and it is way more advanced than before. Again, it is about equipping people through the formal education process. The long cycle would be your primary, secondary and tertiary education and at the sharpest end, your CT portion, which will really be adaptable as the world changes. So you equip your people with the skills, and I would say that part of training isn't just about knowledge, but also to engender leadership. One way to do so is to structurally equip leaders, such as what the Monetary Authority of Singapore (MAS) is doing with the financial organisations through the Financial Scholarship Programme, where MAS co-funds promising financial sector professionals for further study. Such incentives encourage companies to send their local staff for development.

However, one common feedback is that Singaporeans are unwilling to be posted overseas, especially in cities outside the likes of Paris, London or New York. Many Singaporean companies have shared with me that it is a challenge to get Singaporeans to work overseas, especially when the companies are managing a regional or a global market. Generally, I think Singaporeans are as competent as anyone else, we just have to step up. The ones who succeed should then continue to play a role and strengthen and develop other Singaporeans to take over. This has happened in a number of industries such as pharmaceuticals, where a lot of the leaders are Singaporeans. And I don't see why that should not happen elsewhere, because we do have very good people. This is slowly happening, but I think equipping people in terms of education is our strong suit, and we should continue to build on that.

> THE IDEA: **Do not be content with what you have already achieved but always look for opportunities to upgrade your capabilities as well as those of your team members. Investing in their development is a sure way of keeping them invested in you.**

What is your final word of advice for people who are currently in school and considering going into public service?

The first thing is to work out why you think public service is important. Public servants and leaders are expected to have certain qualities. Therefore, you need to reconcile your own values and personal ambitions with the public responsibility entrusted to you. You must also be prepared to go the extra mile. For example, I receive many appeals and requests relating to the Central Provident Fund, which may be difficult to deal with given the legal constraints. While my direct assistance on the particular matter may be limited, I try to link them up with other departments such as the Housing Development Board or Ministry of Social and Family Development, which may assist with the individual's situation as a whole.

As a public servant, you have to think of the situation that the individual is going through and be prepared to go the extra mile. On the policy-making end, you have to be aware of the impact of your policies, and not merely want to score points by coming up with new initiatives. For instance, I have to be aware of the repercussions that may affect small business owners with the tightening of manpower policies. While being ambitious isn't a bad thing, you have to believe that what you are doing is the right, and be very clear about the purpose you are trying to achieve.

> THE IDEA: Be conscious of how the result of a well-intentioned change may have a subsequent negative impact on other issues. Solicit sufficient 360-degree information and feedback before making strategic decisions.

DR WILLIAM WAN
General Secretary
Singapore Kindness Movement

LEAD WITH HUMILITY, THEN WISDOM

DR WILLIAM WAN has been helming the Singapore Kindness Movement (SKM) as its General Secretary since 2011. He also chairs the Prison Fellowship Singapore and the Ethics Committee of Farrer Park Hospital. In addition, he is on the board of several non-profit organisations including the National Kidney Foundation, Singapore Scouts Association, The Bible Society of Singapore and the Singapore Bible College. He also participates in a number of government-linked committees. Over the years, Dr Wan has had a hand in the founding of the Evangelical Fellowship of Singapore and the Lawyers' Christian Fellowship. He played a key role in establishing Operation Mobilisation in Singapore in the 1970s.

Prior to his work with the SKM, Dr Wan was the Managing Director and Senior Vice-President of a psychometric company headquartered in USA. He was also a senior partner of a regional law firm with practices in several cities in Asia, including Shanghai, Tokyo, Ho Chi Minh City, Hanoi, Bangkok and Yangon.

Dr Wan also lived and worked for many years in Washington DC, USA and Ottawa, Canada. During his stint in North America, he was a senior minister of mainline churches in the capital cities, while concurrently a Distinguished Visiting Professor of Asian Studies at Eastern university, Vice-President of a University College, consultant to the police department on race relations and a columnist for a community newspaper.

Dr Wan's interest is wide-ranging as he lives his life in chapters. His academic interest includes law, moral philosophy, theology, biblical studies, religion and ethics. He has contributed numerous articles and essays to various magazines in Singapore and abroad, including *RCMP Gazette, Singapore Law Gazette, Crux, Chinese Churches around the World, Impact, Asian Beacon, Church and Society, Decision, Safety Matters, Today's Parents, Mother and Baby, Today* and *The Straits Times.* He is also author of several books and booklets, including *Pastoral Reflections, More Pastoral Reflections, Test the Spirits* and *5 Amazing Benefits of Being Kind.* Additonally, he contributed chapters to several books including an article on "Crime" in Law and Justice in Singapore and one on "Kindness" in Serving God's Community.

His community work in North America was acknowledged by the Solicitor-General of Ontario, who conferred him the SG of Ontario Award for Crime Prevention. He was also awarded the Ottawa Board of Police Commissioners' Commendation for Police-Community Education. In the USA, he was recognised for his contribution to the Equal Opportunity Employment Program by the Department of Transport, Washington DC.

In 2011, Dr Wan received the Active Ager Award from the Council for Third Age. At 61, he started fulfilling his bucket list which includes skydiving, scuba diving, snipe racing and rock climbing.

Dr Wan continues to live an active life in his role as General Secretary of the SKM. He speaks regularly about kindness and related values several times a month to a cross-section of audiences at educational institutions, corporate retreats, churches and thematic conferences. He continues to write on subjects close to his heart and mind. He has been happily married for 45 years and has three children and three teenage grandchildren.

LEADING YOURSELF

How did you begin your career and how did it lead up to you now being the General Secretary for the Singapore Kindness Movement?

My career started when I enrolled at the Singapore Bible College after secondary school. At the end of my first year, I became a pastor. In a sense, I started very young. Before I was 20, I was a college student and pastored a church at the same time. When I completed college, I didn't think that I was intellectually or academically equipped. In order to prepare myself for the role I wanted to play in this world, I decided to enrol at the University of Singapore. That was when I started doing Law. I continued as a pastor while I was doing law.

In my second year of law school, I got married. I was also the chairman of the Varsity Christian Fellowship for two consecutive years, which was an extremely proactive student organisation. After completing my law degree, I declined an invitation to join the Law faculty. Instead, I practiced law for a few years and left for Canada in response to a call to teach in a theological setting. I did my graduate school in Canada and spent three years in Vancouver and Ottawa. I returned armed with a couple of graduate degrees and taught at a theological centre in Singapore for three years while pastoring Bartley Christian Church at the same time.

What were some of your achievements in church and community building efforts?

In Ottawa, I was heavily involved in community work as a consultant to the Ottawa Police Department where I created a programme for the police department on cross-cultural understanding. In those days, the police officers were primarily white, Irish- and French-speaking Canadians who were very ignorant of cultures beyond the Catholic-French culture and quite desperate to understand the culture of these new immigrants in order to police them effectively.

After this, I went to Toronto and became vice-president of a university college and continued as a pastor as well. One of the things I did there was to provide leadership in embarking on the process of converting a bible college into an university college.

From there I moved on to Washington DC where I was senior minister of the Chinese Community Church of Washington D.C. In my third year there, I succeeded in bringing the whites, Asians and blacks together in one church through a shared ministry with the Mt Vernon United Methodist Church across the road. Because Washington D.C. was and still is a very racially-divided city in spite of the fact that it is the nation's capital, what I did was reported on the front page of the *Washington Post* one Easter Sunday morning.

What led you to the Singapore Kindness Movement?

We returned to Singapore in 1996, and I pastored my home church (Bartley Christian Church) for a couple of years before I went back to practice law for almost 10 years. I retired when I was 60 and decided to take up a position as the managing director and senior vice-president of a psychometric company which I ran for four years.

I was connected to the SKM while I was managing the psychometric business. I attended a couple of their annual general meetings and got to know some of the board members. One day, I had lunch with the leadership of SKM, and was asked if I would be interested in driving the movement, and as they say, the rest is history.

Who were some of your leadership role models? What did you learn from them?

Most of my role models were older people, probably because I started young. In the late 1970s, I was working very closely with Dr Benjamin Chew, Professor Khoo Oon Teik and Mr Goh Ewe Kheng, among others. We founded the Evangelical Fellowship of Singapore (EFOS). Dr Chew was the president and the other two were vice-presidents. I was the general secretary. Professor Khoo was a very eminent specialist in a number of medical disciplines, as well as a lay churchman who provided a lot of leadership both to his church and to other organisations. He was also, among other things, the founder of the National Kidney Foundation. I had the privilege of working with him to bring together Christians of all denominations to work together. I learnt many qualities of leadership from him. For example, he treated me with tremendous respect despite my youth. He honoured me by considering me to be his co-worker and colleague. He taught me that leadership is about accepting people for who they are. It is about being able to work with different people at different levels without making people feel any less than who they are. Professor Khoo taught me to invest and believe in a person's potential.

> THE IDEA: Leaders accept others for who they are
> and are able to see beyond differences in others
> and look for their latent potential.

Were there any other leaders who inspired you?

Dr Benjamin Chew taught me about personal discipline. He was a very active medical doctor, and yet he studied Greek and Hebrew on his own. He was also able to expound scriptures in a very powerful way. A lot of my leadership training came from the context of my being a Christian. Dr Chew's faith, care and compassion for people rubbed off on me. I did not grow up with a father as he was an absentee father and passed away early in my life. Dr Chew and the other honoured elders of the church were fathers to me, and yet they treated me as an equal when we worked together. I learnt a lot of leadership qualities from them – humility, discipline, compassion and respect for others. Mr Goh taught me a great deal about voluntarism and generosity.

When I was abroad, I met other senior people who taught me a lot about leadership. In Canada, one of my professors was Dr Jim Houston. He was a geographer from Oxford who founded Regent College in Vancouver, British Columbia. Another professor was the late Klaus Bockmuehl, a Swiss-German. These two men were my professors when I was doing graduate studies at Regent College. They were extremely good teachers who gave a lot of attention to individual students and invested their time in us. I did my PhD primarily because of Professor Bockmuehl. Every year for 10 years since I graduated, he would call to ask if I had started on my PhD. He taught me what it means to be a good teacher. The key to being a good teacher is about investing in the potential of your students, being there for your students and treating them as individuals with their own unique strengths. Professor Houston taught me to mature with grace. "It is not about aging," he said, "it is about sage-ing." He is a good example of what active aging is all about. He is highly disciplined and would travel around the world to communicate his passion even into his 80s. He continues to lecture and write and is still very intellectually sharp even as he pushes into his 90s.

I should also add that in my last year of law school at the University of Singapore, Prof Tommy Koh was the dean and he had a great influence on me. He taught a Criminal Justice module and his deep sense of justice and compassion for all rubbed off on me. He believed in my potential and invited me to join the faculty. My interest in working alongside offenders to help reintegrate them into society as contributing citizens is largely due to his influence.

What guidelines or principles do you live by as a leader?

The first is humility. On my travels, I often make it a point to visit local cemeteries to remind myself of my mortality. No matter how powerful or wealthy, it's only temporary. I don't see any reason for human beings to be arrogant or to suppress or oppress anyone. We should treat one another with equal respect because we are all made of the same mortal stuff. Humility is my first principle because life is transient.

> THE IDEA: Do not step on others for your own gain. We will all be stepped upon when we are six feet under. Humility makes all the difference in a respected leader.

What is the second principle?

My second principle is wisdom. I think wisdom goes beyond just having knowledge, it must come from the hard knocks of life, from active aging and experience. Every experience is precious, not just the positive ones. Everyone goes through difficult times. There is wisdom in experiencing the rough side of life, and we should not deny ourselves that. Consider it a privilege to experience difficult times because it makes us more resilient. If we do not know anything about the dark and painful side of life, we may not appreciate what we have. Wisdom is the ability to use our knowledge to make sound judgments.

What was the final principle?

The third principle is to be holistically fit. We must keep ourselves fit intellectually, physically and emotionally. Being fit emotionally means that we have to know ourselves and be aware of what our strengths are. It is also about not trying to be like someone else. We should play to our strengths. Always be ready to concede that there are better and smarter people; be content but not complacent. We must also be socially fit. This means being able to relate to people from diverse backgrounds and to walk comfortably with both kings and paupers. Of course, we must also be spiritually fit. I practice my faith tradition with passion and seek to be compassionate to all regardless of race or religion. Faith gives an additional dimension to life so that we don't live mechanically without a sense of mystery and wonder.

THE IDEA: Keeping a holistic fitness regime of emotional intelligence, embracing diversity of thought and ideas and having strong faith keeps a leader sharp.

How old are you and how do you manage your time?

I just turned 68. On typical days, I get up at 5am in the morning to do some reading, I pray and meditate, and I reflect and contemplate. I do my workout and have breakfast at 7am. I will usually be at work at 8am unless I have a breakfast meeting. I also try to schedule meetings during meal times because those are times when I can also catch up with people. I try to have dinner with my wife as often as I can.

I attend a lot of meetings with partners these days, and support my partners in their events because I believe in the maxim, "Do unto others what you want others to do unto you." My days are long.

Before we go to bed, my wife and I often like to watch an old movie. I usually get to bed about 12 midnight.

On Saturdays, I try to take time out to drive around the nooks and corners of Singapore with my wife. On Sundays, I am usually preaching at one church or another. I try to spend my Sunday afternoons at my club enjoying the jacuzzi and the steam bath once a week.

> THE IDEA: In addition to the discipline that we give to our work routine, we should also dedicate a sacred amount of time for our loved ones and not take those commitments for granted because of work obligations.

How can one manage when they fall or go through adversities?

I try to live out the theology of grace and mercy. Grace is to receive what I do not deserve and mercy, the flip side of grace, is not to receive what I deserve. Either way, I live with gratitude. So I believe that all things happen to me for a higher purpose. When adversities come my way, I accept it as part of being equipped for better things. They are just roadblocks, not dead ends. I have to slow down, reflect on what happened, learn from it, get up and move on. You don't wait for people to come and pick you up; they may never come. I have faith in God and so I look to God. I seek his strength and wisdom and move on with gratitude and positivity.

Having reflected on what transpired, I believe that we should not blame others for the negative events in our lives. It takes two to tango; you must also have contributed to the problem, even if to a small degree. You learn from it, you pick yourself up and you forgive. If I make a mistake, I must forgive myself. If others made the mistake, I must forgive them. If you don't forgive people, you are going to kill yourself – a lack of forgiveness hurts only yourself and not the other person.

I've also learnt to reinvent myself and to adapt. I believe in creation but evolutionary theories provide important lessons for me. One of them is that we survive because we adapt. We can only survive if we learn to adapt because every situation is different. You adapt and find ways and means to excel; you have to look at yourself in terms of your strengths, press forward and do your best. I think that's how I was able to live my life reasonably successfully.

THE IDEA: **It's easy to blame others for our setbacks but in doing so we will never grow and learn from these lessons in life. Forgive others and it will set you free from the shackles of past mistakes.**

What was your most effective leadership development experience?

I have been privileged to have had leaders who invested in me because they could see my potential. Many of them were much older than I was. They were very prominent in their own fields and yet took the time to mentor me. The mentoring was informal, mostly while I was working for or with them; they would share their views and ideas over a meal or a cup of coffee. Sometimes, I would have my learning moment during a debriefing session. I am essentially a curious person and read a fair bit. I enjoyed asking questions and picking their brains.

More importantly, they empowered and trusted me to carry out a task or a responsibility. They gave me permission to make decisions, and yes, permission to fail. That was where I learnt a great deal about leadership – I learnt by failing and with their gentle coaching, to find a better way to do it. I also learnt from my critics and detractors, especially honest ones who were not afraid to speak their minds without fear or favour.

> THE IDEA: Dedicate 30 minutes a day to have a coffee break with a junior in the organisation. The mutual insights gained and informal mentoring time would be a great energy booster.

LEADING OTHERS

What makes a good leader? What makes you a good leader?

It's up to others to say whether I am a good leader. A good leader should love the people he leads, believe in the people he leads and enjoy being with them. You lead because you care and not just to promote yourself. You lead because you really believe in what you do, you believe that your mission is something worth investing in. A good leader must be passionate about what he does, and this passion will rub off onto others. Your followers are also more likely to follow you when you are sincere, especially when they also know you care for them and that you are not going to use them. When people realise that they are also the beneficiaries of whatever good you are going to do and that they can participate in it, they are more likely to follow you. You might be a leading boat in a fleet, but when the tide rises, you have to make sure that every other boat following you rises with you.

Always give credit to your team instead of to yourself. Camaraderie is very important. We also lead by example; a leader has to walk his talk. A leader will not ask his people to do something that he would not do. Servant leadership is not just a nice word, it means that I am really interested in asking my team how I can serve you and make you a better person. It is not about me, it's about us.

> THE IDEA: **Passion for your mission and compassion for your team are a potent combination for effective leadership.**

Our team once had a retreat to come up with our core values. The first core value is synergy. Synergy is about teamwork – together, we can do much more. It's also about harnessing our energy according to our strengths. The next value is kinship. Kinship is about friendship; we are like a family. We spend more time together during the waking hours on work days than with our own families. If you are dragging yourself to work because you don't like someone, then you are in trouble. The third value is mindset. Mindset involves positivity, abundance and a can-do spirit. We must be willing to experiment, and as a leader, I must allow people the opportunity to fail because it is in failing that they learn. I am not afraid of the team failing, what I am afraid of is people covering up their mistakes. It is necessary for people to learn from their mistakes. A positive mindset means to see everything as an opportunity, including failures. They are just challenges and not problems.

Is there a difference between a good manager and a good leader?
Managing is akin to shifting the furniture. You can shift and move the furniture around to make it look better. Leadership, to me, is

not about moving the furniture. It is about recreating and thinking about how best to use the furniture in many different ways. It is also about how to strengthen what you have so that it can last longer and be more useful. Leadership is more than just managing, it goes to the very core of making a difference and leaving things better than when you first found them. Finally, a leader must be optimistic on top of being realistic.

THE IDEA: **Don't just shift the furniture around, your job as a leader is to reinvent and recreate new possibilities.**

How do you build an effective team and nurture it?

I think building a team is about spending time with your team leaders and your team. I think understanding and getting to know them more, finding out what their aspirations are and finding ways to fulfil their aspirations allows me to nurture them as a team.

We come together to play a game called "Focus on You". It is a time for them to talk about themselves, and we identify a number of items that they can speak freely about. We can also discuss things that we want to know about them. When they are expressing themselves, we observe them and figure out what makes them tick, what are some of their pet peeves, and so on. We want to avoid things they do not like, and do things that we know they will appreciate. I think affirmation is very important. Affirmation is done not only through monetary terms, but also through giving them a pat on the back and taking them out for a coffee. All these are very important to build self-confidence and a sense that they are noticed, valued and appreciated. Many of my team members are young people who use WhatsApp and other social media platforms, and I participate alongside them and use appropriate words of affirmation. Sometimes, I will also give them a challenge and then help them to accomplish it.

The nurturing of a team must begin internally. They must first feel good about themselves. Then, they have a different perspective of what they do. Their contribution is part of a bigger picture. For example, the SKM is not just about smiling at others and giving up seats on public transport, it is about nation-building through creating pro-social human behaviour.

THE IDEA: Experiment with a "Focus on You" session with the team but make sure that they are doing the talking and not you. Look for opportunities of positive affirmation whenever possible. Give them a bigger mission than just doing a job.

Is there a leadership challenge you have encountered that showcases you as a leader?

In law, I have a range of experience from commercial business to litigation and from defending offenders to being a rainmaker of the firm. I did most of my criminal defence work pro bono and volunteered to work for people who could not afford a lawyer.

One of the guys I defended was a young man who was alleged to have committed murder. He was charged for rioting and murder, which carried a death sentence. I looked at the situation and I believed that the young man did not do it. I spent a lot of personal time investigating the scene and made applications to the AG Chambers to reduce the charge to affray, which was declined. My client was in remand for nine months. When he came to the trial, the charge was actually reduced to affray and he was sentenced to one year. It was important to me because I believed in him and I persistently lobbied for them to reduce the charge. I was prepared to go to trial still believing that they would reduce the charge. To me, it is not about the money you make. In this case, it is about saving a life. Today this young man is married with kids, and the last thing he told me was that he had gone to Australia to pursue a degree. For me, my calling to practice law was to bring about justice. Because I believe in justice, I persevered and eventually reached a just conclusion I wanted. It is always a leadership challenge not to give up no matter how tough the journey.

In the church context, I've always believed in racial harmony. To be able to bring a Washington D.C. church to a point where they embraced the whites, the blacks and the Asians together in one church was a dream of a lifetime. I started with a Chinese church with a congregation that was growing too fast for its church size. Across the road was a much larger church with a dwindling congregation. I negotiated a shared ministry and consolidated the two. They were resistant initially, and it was not easy, but we managed to bring the white congregation and Asian congregation together. Some African immigrants also joined us. I had a vision of what was possible and although I had many detractors, I was focused on getting there.

In Ottawa, I was involved in resettling some of the Cambodian and Vietnamese refugees and later helped to start the Cambodian church. There were two young Cambodian guys whom I mentored. One of them is now a widely published professor of political science in Canada and was a Fellow at the Institute of Southeast Asian Studies. The other wrote a couple of books and is now in Cambodia doing social work. These people were initially refugees and did not have much education, but I set up a committee of friends and started a church for them. We raised money and saw to some of their needs. To me, this is what the church is about. It is not just about religion or growing the numbers – it is about having the faith to make a difference in people's lives. Even though the church as a social entity has failed in many ways and many people are turned off by it, I still believe in it because it is a biblical way to gather people of faith to make a difference in people's lives. In fact, we need more bright examples of what churches can do for the world in the wake of loss of confidence in organised religion.

In the academic context, when I was teaching in Canada and the US, I worked with international students and professors from other countries. A Japanese scientist came to Ottawa and we embraced and accept him into our community. This is remarkable because of the historical animosity between the Chinese and Japanese that does not seem to have completely disappeared. We opened our home to him, his wife and child for two months when they were waiting to go back to Tokyo. He was so touched that when he returned to Tokyo, he opened his home to Chinese students as well. We lost touch for many years but recently we reconnected and he wrote to say that they have our family picture on their piano all these years. They are planning to visit us. Leadership is being unafraid to risk misunderstanding and to inspire emulation of what is good.

THE IDEA: When you do good and see it then paid forward to others, it is the start of a movement. Kindness always breeds kindness.

LEADING THE ORGANISATION

How was Singapore Kindness Movement (SKM) started?
The SKM came about as a result of Singapore's former prime minister Mr Goh Chok Tong's speech on a gracious society in 1996. By 2000, the SKM was founded. The SKM then subsumed the early courtesy campaign started by the first prime minister, Mr Lee Kuan Yew.

The SKM is about changing behaviour. When I came on board, it was a small organisation despite having been around for about 12 years. There were just five or six people in the team and I realised that there was so much more we could do. At the time, we were given some funding on a yearly basis. It is hard to plan for the future when you only have a year's supply of money, and as such, I requested for at least a three-year grant of funds. The second issue was manpower – we took our time and looked for the right people. They have to be passionate and fit well with the existing team. We now have a team of 20 people.

We also needed partners in both the government and the private sectors because we could not do everything on our own. We needed to multiply our effectiveness by securing partners. We wanted partners who would share part of the costs, and we've found partners who believe in kindness. One of our newest partners is Coca-Cola. They paid for everything in creating the viral video "Happiness from the Skies", with which we thanked the foreign workers who built our infrastructure. The Ministry of Education is also our partner and we work with them to implement their Value in Action (VIA) programme, which is part of their citizenship and character education curriculum.

To me, fostering kindness has to be a people's movement, it has to be owned by people. We can only change one person at a time because kindness begins with one person. One kind act will have a positive ripple effect. We hope that, in time, we will reach a tipping point where the majority of people are practicing kind acts. This will then exert subtle social pressure on people who are averse to it. I think this is the only way to change.

What are some of the challenges to this movement?

I have written articles and some people have chosen to either not read them, or to ride on other people's comments in a social media context and attack me without caring to read what I've written. If they have read my articles, it is obvious that they have misunderstood what I've written and there is nothing I can do about it. I look at it from another perspective – 90% of the people are open to listening. For the 5% who disagree with reasons and care to write about it in a civil manner, I do my best to respond to them. For the other 5% who simply attack with malice, I can't do much about it so I leave it and do not take it personally. I press on and do what I believe is the right thing to do. The challenge is not to allow the minority to shut you up, but to be thick-skinned enough not to take these attacks personally.

The other challenge is that the constant aspects of the movement are very hard to pin down as we are a dynamic society with a rapidly changing population. I believe in working slowly and steadily. The challenge is also to resist thinking that we can get instant results. We have to look at it in the long-term. We are talking about changing behaviours and cultures and it takes a long time to develop such. Another challenge is to measure kindness. We cannot measure kindness effectively; there are a lot of factors that might give rise to an inaccurate measurement. The encouragement for us is to hear people speak of the effectiveness of our reminders which made them stop to do a kind act.

There is one more challenge, and that is to change people's perception that we are a government agency or mouthpiece. We are not. We are given a grant to do the work of fostering kindness which is much needed, but we are a non-profit, non-government organisation and a charity with an Institution of Public Character status. We are accountable to a council of ordinary citizens. Just because we receive a grant and have the prime minister as our patron does not make us a government mouthpiece.

> THE IDEA: No matter how well a job you do, you will
> have detractors who do not value-add. It's best to
> ignore them and not take the criticism personally.

How do you convince partners to get on board?

My fundamental belief is that almost all of us are innately kind. We may not be able to define kindness, but every one of us knows what kindness and unkindness are.

Our partners are people who resonate with what we do. They know that there is a need for kindness and that we have to do something about it. For example, the National Environment Agency is very concerned about cleanliness. When people dirty their surroundings, they are being unkind to the environment and their behaviour is also inconsiderate, which means that they are unkind to users of the common space. These behaviours are anti-social. Pro-social behaviour, on the other hand, exhibitare values within kindness. Graciousness encompasses respect, thoughtfulness, being appreciative and considerate. When you break down all the big issues, they boil down to simple human behaviour that is driven by kindness.

We work with the Singapore Hotel Association because they believe in rendering good service. Good service is often portrayed through gracious behaviour such as remembering guests' names, giving them warm welcomes and fond farewells. We work with the association by giving awards to their service staff to affirm such gracious services. Graciousness on the part of guests is also recognised and appreciated. Kindness Is a two-way street.

The annual award ceremony reminds them to step up, start, show and share kindness. It is not enough to just believe in it. You have to do something about it. With more people doing so, we can reach a tipping point. We also encourage them to nominate gracious guests and recognise them because graciousness goes both ways.

> THE IDEA: Leaders constantly have to look beyond their own boundaries and explore synergies with partners to achieve win-win results.

What is your final advice to your mentee who wants to be a community leader like you?

I think wanting to be a community leader is a very noble desire. The first and most important thing I would say to this person is to go out and spend some time with the people. Don't even think of yourself as a leader but go and volunteer, and learn about the work. Before you can be a leader, you have to be a follower. A good leader is a good follower. Learn all you can from the people who have been there and done that, and then be energised by the environment you are immersed in. Do you really enjoy it? Do you feel the passion growing inside you? Does being with people whom you care about energise you? If so, then you are very likely to be cut out for that kind of work. Get involved and grow in your leadership. Don't expect to become a leader overnight. In a way, you'll grow to become a leader. The people around you will recognise you one, and they will gravitate around you and gradually push you into leadership positions. You cannot just appoint yourself as a leader.

> THE IDEA: To lead well, one must first be a good follower. Self-appointment is never as convincing as a group nomination.

ALICIA YI
Managing Director and Co-Leader Asia Pacific
Korn Ferry

EMBRACE DIVERSITY

ALICIA YI brings to Korn Ferry a strong human capital consultancy background. In her current position as Managing Director, Asia Pacific Consumer Market, she works closely with teams globally and throughout the region to engage with top clients across the globe to build and develop their leadership teams.

Prior to joining Korn Ferry, Ms Yi served at another leading executive search firm where she led the Singapore office as the managing partner. There, she built up the consumer practice, driving key accounts in the fast moving consumer goods (FMCG), retail and hospitality sectors to develop global key client relationships. Ms Yi also established and led the regional human resources functional practice with a team of HR specialists across key countries, building a significant practice.

Prior to search, Ms Yi built and led her own consulting business, focusing on HR strategy. Earlier, she was with Towers Perrin as head of the compensation practice in Singapore and Chicago, and the international HR manager with Swiss Bank Corporation based in Zurich.

Ms Yi is an active member of the Young President Organization (YPO). She is also a frequent speaker on leadership, gender diversity and human capital strategy. Ms Yi received a bachelor's degree of arts from Northwestern University, Illinois

LEADING YOURSELF

What were your early career aspirations prior to joining Korn Ferry?

I started my career in Chicago after I graduated from Northwestern University. I was in my first job at a management consulting firm, Towers Perrin, in Chicago for about five years in the late 1980s. At the time, consulting and investment banking were the two really hot industries. Having studied economics, the only thing I wanted was to become a legitimate businesswoman. That wasn't the path that a lot of girls in my generation took, although the idea of a "career woman" was starting to take root. It was very important for me to become a career woman, but I didn't know what that journey meant. All I wanted was a profession that I was proud of and that I wanted to be a part of.

Another thing I wanted was an international career, it was something I felt compelled to have even when I was young and living in Korea then. I was very lucky that my parents ended up moving to the States and bringing me with them. Even in the US, I wanted to see the world – being in the US wasn't enough for me. When I had the opportunity to join the Swiss Bank Corporation, the title of my job at the time was International Compensation Manager. I was attracted to the title "international" because I thought it would expose me to the world. Six months into that job in Chicago, they asked me to move to Switzerland. At that time, I had been married for a year and as my husband was getting an MBA, he could not move with me to Switzerland and we had to live apart for two years. It was challenging from a personal standpoint, but it was a fantastic experience – I had the chance to experience Europe first-hand, to experience the nuances of different countries, different provinces, different business issues, and so I got my "international".

> THE IDEA: A leader's journey may take you beyond your comfort zone and involve personal sacrifices, but the experience truly broadens your outlook and profile.

What happened after that first international career stint?

I moved back to Chicago and I was itching to have another international assignment. I was very keen to experience Asia again because I was born in Korea but I did not always experience Asia as I was growing up. I was at a dinner party with my ex-colleagues from Towers Perrin and I told them that I would love to do another stint in Asia. The following week, I got a call from the global head of compensation practice within Towers Perrin, who offered me a job in Singapore to run their compensation practice.

After five years with them, I then decided to try my luck starting my own firm, and I established Carrots Consulting. At the time, during the dot.com days in 2000, Towers Perrin was turning down a lot of dot.com clients who needed new HR policies, incentive programmes, stock option plans, etc. They were just too small for Towers Perrin and I thought that was a niche that I could fill.

What did you gain from the experience of running your own consulting business?

There are a lot of things that I've gained from that particular experience. One, I used to feel that the clients were hiring the firm when they hired me and I was just representing the firm. I was thus surprised when a lot of my ex client companies such as OCBC, NOL and DBS bank told me that they just wanted to work with me. We actually beat out some of the global players to win some of these global assignments because the clients trusted me with the projects. At Carrots Consulting, I had fewer clients but really dedicated myself to those clients in the best way possible and gave it my all.

The second thing I learnt from that experience is that I am more of a corporate person than an entrepreneur. When you start a firm on your own, there is no such thing as standing still. You either grow the business and continue to evolve or you shut it down – there is nothing in between. It is a challenging and balancing act to sustain a relatively small business. What I missed then was a global network and global resources. I've always appreciated working for international companies and working internationally. I enjoy working with people from all over the world and I like having that access which was missing in a small firm set-up.

> THE IDEA: Your personal brand and charisma can have a greater effect on your clients than the corporate brand. When setting up his or her own company, a leader will often gain a great sense of autonomy but lose personal time, a global network and resources.

From being an entrepreneur and going back to corporate life, what were the transition points?

By then, I had been a compensation specialist and compensation consultant for about 15 years in total. I knew the subject matter really well, but it was time for a change. That was when I got a call from Heidrick & Struggles, a global executive search firm, and decided to take the risk and make the change. It was the best career switch I've ever done.

That career took off quite fast after the first year. In the first year, I was just knocking on doors and meeting as many people as I possibly could. I did not have anything to show for but it was the second year that my career started taking off. I became partner of Heidrick & Struggles in my third year, and in the fifth year, I became the office-managing partner and was one of the biggest billing partners. I knew that I had found something that really suited me, that played on my strengths and built on my past experiences, but that also gave me a kind of renewal, new zest and new passion in my career.

> THE IDEA: At the mid-point mark in your leadership journey, it may potentially be a great move for a leader to make a transition into a different industry, function or geography to add new zest and passion.

And finally, you made it to Korn Ferry?

It was a huge exodus from Heidrick & Struggles to Korn Ferry – over 100 partners made the move. Korn Ferry was on a journey to reinvent their business, which attracted many of us to make the move because the search business is evolving and as a professional, you also have to evolve and find ways to stay relevant in the new world. With LinkedIn and a number of other technologies available now, you need to find different anchors that will bring in clients who are looking above and beyond what a database has to offer.

THE IDEA: Despite current successes, leaders cannot simply relish the status quo but must constantly spot upcoming trends that affect careers and businesses. It takes foresight to transition before the growth curve declines.

Briefly tell me about your current role at Korn Ferry.

I am currently the head of the consumer industry practice for Asia Pacific. I engage with clients in the sector and service them globally and regionally the best we can.

I am also a member of the firm's Board and CEO services, which is essentially the Board's practice. I am also one of the champions in the firm pushing to get more women into the Board, which allows me to marry my professional passion with my personal passion.

THE IDEA: Great leaders go beyond managing their individual work functions and often identify cross-functional projects that they are passionate to lead in.

What are some of your life lessons on leading yourself?

There are a couple of things that I find are fundamental to leading yourself. They are knowing yourself and, to a certain extent, accepting yourself. I have always grown up with quintessential Asian family values where working hard and succeeding are very important. I lived with a lot of pressure, but that also meant that I was quite hard on myself. I expected a lot from myself and you inherit the values that your parents instil upon you. It cuts both ways. That's something I had to really learn as a grown-up – when do I switch from being self-critical to being self-accepting? It takes a lot of self-reflection and I see that often with Asians and with women in general.

To me, knowing the things that you are not good at is just as important as recognising your strengths. When you are doing your job, you want to maximise your strengths and figure out how valuable they are to your environment. And then, figure out what you can do to have a multiplier effect on the areas you are good at. I then look for team members who are complementary and can support me in areas that I am not very good at. I am very open about my strengths and weaknesses, and I am also very open about their strengths and weaknesses. It does not mean that you are giving up on areas that you are weaker in, you need to understand your own limitations because you cannot be good at everything and need to accept that. Once you have self-acceptance, you are a better person as you realise that you don't have to be perfect.

> THE IDEA: Before leading others, one has to lead
> themselves well and to do so requires a high level
> of self-awareness and self-acceptance. Accept that
> you have limits as well as weaknesses, which you can
> leverage on others to support you.

Who are some of your leadership role models? What did you learn from them?

I don't think there are single role models whom I want to be like, but there are different leaders and mentors I've had throughout my career who have inspired me. I also looked at people who are not good leaders and managers and learnt from watching them as well. I tend to analyse them by breaking them down into qualities that I admire or do not like – what makes a person work or not work as a leader, manager or professional.

What leadership qualities do you exercise regularly?

Integrity is one of the key factors that I always come down to. You don't expect a person to be perfect, but you appreciate it when you get an honest answer about themselves or the situation.

The second aspect is diversity. If I look at my team across the region as well as in Singapore, I've made a considerable effort to have diversity in the team. In my immediate team in Singapore, we have French, Belgium and Australian staff working with the Singaporean staff. At Korn Ferry, we have all nationalities represented across Asia Pacific in different markets. It's very consistent with what my clients are doing. Although it is more challenging initially because of differences in culture and style, we found that the diversity stimulates thinking. A homogeneous team may be efficient at first, but it does not create new thinking – it does not challenge the status quo, and innovation can sometimes get stifled. From a leadership standpoint, being able to manage diverse groups of people is a very important skill set, and not everyone has it.

> THE IDEA: A leader's temptation is to have a team that it is easy to get consensus and gel with but that can easily lead to groupthink and substandard ideas. Dare to pick team members that don't quite fit the mould to trigger discomfort within the team. It is the sand that irritates the oyster which forms the pearl.

How would you develop this diversity in thought within your team?

Being exposed early on in my career to many different nationalities definitely helped. Unless they are exposed to it, most people tend to stick to what they know. They have a fear of the unknown. If you look at a lot of great companies, they move their talents across geographies and functions from very early on in their careers. I think that's how a lot of companies are now developing truly international talent and global citizens who can embrace diversity from a natural development perspective. It's something that is very hard to learn in the classrooms.

> THE IDEA: Put into place a mobility programme to move your talents across new regions, countries and functions to expose them to different ways of doing things. A successful career is not simply about moving up the ranks but also involves well-rounded exposure to the entire supply chain.

Do you see that quality among our youths today?

One of the things that I think is a missed opportunity in Singapore is that you don't see that many students, be it high school or college, who work as waiters in restaurants, busboys and car-washers. In many other countries, a lot of students work. Money is the least of all that they've gained. These experiences teach you work ethics and that money does not fall from the sky. When you have to work really hard for a reward, you have a greater appreciation for it. These experiences also help us focus on the things we want in the future. You don't realise how difficult it is to be a service staff unless you've done it. There are so many life lessons that I've learnt, and I really do think that the students in Singapore are under so much pressure to do well academically that there's just no room to fit in a part-time job.

> THE IDEA: Expose the young to seemingly menial labour to train their empathy, strong work ethics and the virtue of not taking things for granted.

What's your impression of Singaporean leaders/ managers in general?

Singaporeans are very good at the entry level and at rising to the middle management, but lose out to other nationalities at the very top leadership roles in a multinational company. A lot of Singaporeans are very comfortable being in Singapore because it's a utopia and it's very comfortable compared to other developing countries. Because Singaporeans don't take risks early on in their careers, it hurts them in the long run. I took risks going to Switzerland alone without a single friend, and in coming to Singapore. It was difficult at first, but it was one of those experiences that shaped me. Now, I feel very comfortable with my friends and colleagues of different nationalities. I would encourage all young people to travel not just as a tourist, but to work and live in a different country.

> THE IDEA: As a leader, encourage risk-taking among your junior talents and be an appropriate sounding board when required.

Was there a period of time when you had to go through an adversity and when you stood up as a leader?

This has something to do with being a woman. I remember when I was first appointed as an office-managing partner at my previous employer, it was a really big achievement for me but I was always a little bit afraid to step into that role. I met one of the first visitors to the Singapore office. He was a colleague from Australia and he inadvertently mentioned that I did not look like an office managing director. I was taken aback, and my initial instinct was to become a shrinking violet – was he saying that I am a fake? I thought about what he said and realised that my firm's Asia Pacific leadership team consisted of 90% white males and shockingly, I was the only female and I was one of the youngest in the firm.

I got to the next stage of my emotion – I was proud of myself. I became the first young female office-managing partner. That jolted me into thinking about how I was going to define my leadership. Initially, my insecurities made me feel like I had to be like them to prove myself. But I realised that if I was going to do my role exactly like my predecessor or another white male, then what was the point of having diversity in the leadership team? That was not me, and I wanted to be a new kind of leader who was different and who would inspire other kinds of leaders. A leader is not a one-dimensional image; leaders can look and feel different. This brings us back to diversity.

> THE IDEA: Even if you are filling the "very big shoes" of another leader who has left, it does not mean that you need to be another "mini me". Discover how you are going to define your own leadership brand and lead with authenticity.

LEADING OTHERS

What did you do to cultivate your unique leadership brand?

I hired a coach to work with me to define my leadership style, my brand as a leader and the legacy I wanted to leave. That entire exercise also meant that I looked at the office to figure out what was missing – why did I agree to take on this role? What did I want to change? Part of it was introducing laughter in the office because my predecessor was tense and serious. I didn't like that because I don't believe that you bring out the best in people when they are afraid. I made a considerable effort to change all that. There are many things I did in the office to completely change the culture.

I would have regular lunches with the secretarial staff to understand their concerns. I created a suggestion box for people who had ideas on how to change the office culture. For the more senior professional groups, I encouraged them to have a regular meeting to come up with activities that could be fun both socially and in terms of work. Even for weekly office meetings, we always start by seeing how people are feeling so that we can be more empathetic. I started laughing, and my team started laughing, there were more happy vibes. We start our week with laughter, jokes and care before we start with the serious numbers in business.

THE IDEA: Refrain from bringing the "bossman" façade to the office and instead allow your team to see your authentic self as you mutually build trust over time. This is especially so with a Gen-Y workforce that appreciates informality and a "boss as friend" approach.

What is the business case for bringing fun and laughter to the workplace?

The way I see it, every person has an emotional need and this need has to be matched while in an organisation, be it in terms of your ambition or whether the culture fits you. I believe that being in an emotionally positive state brings out the best in you. When your emotional needs are met, you can then elevate yourself to think about the business, the strategy and how to be better at what you do. As the leader, you have to create and work in an environment where people's emotions are respected and acknowledged.

We had a situation where we had to fire a staff because of trust issues. I had the job of firing her, watching her pack and walk out the door, and also to announce to the whole office what had just happened. This occured just as I was trying hard to create a warm, loving and fun office environment. I had to have my staff trust me that it was the right thing to do. What I am most proud of is how I try to consciously evolve myself to be a good leader and not just a good professional – not just being good at what I do, but also from an organisational culture standpoint, to champion and model the type of environment I would want to work in.

THE IDEA: Engaging with your team members does not just create a "feel good" atmosphere. Research shows that engaged employees are more productive. They are more profitable, more customer-focused, safer and more likely to withstand temptations to leave the organisation.

As an established female leader, do you think that there are certain unique characteristics or challenges of being a female leader in a multinational organisation? How should one navigate them?

In many companies, there are a lot of women at the professional and middle-management level, but the number of women drops dramatically when you get to director, vice president and senior vice president levels. I think the issue is multifaceted. The fact that women bear children has something to do with it because the child-bearing age is often when you are at the height of your career. You have to slow down while your male colleagues are accelerating. There's always maternal instinct and family responsibility that forces women to have a bit more work-life balance and they might take a country role instead of a regional role because they don't want to travel so much. Whether you are single or married, you are challenged. That forces you to take a slower track at the height of your career and make some career sacrifices.

Women often have some self-doubt. I think it's partly because they don't see enough female role models. They don't always dare to see themselves as a leader, to ask for a role, negotiate for a higher package or say that they want a global role. A lot of women are very shy about their own ambition, it's like ambition is a bad thing. This is not the case for men, where ambition is seen as a good thing. When you say a female colleague is ambitious, it has negative connotations. Women expect other women to be nurturing; when they are described as aggressive, it's not a positive trait.

The Harvard Business School conducted an experiement where two case studies of CEOs were presented to their students. The only difference between these two case studies was that one was a female while the other was a male. While the male CEO was described as having very positive attributes such as a strong leadership style and being strategic, the female CEO's leadership style was described with many negative adjectives. The response from the students on the leadership styles and the effectiveness of the two CEOs was very different despite there being no difference between the two case studies except for their gender. There are a lot of biases that are built in to how people view women in leadership compared to men. These biases didn't come from male students only, they also came from female students. I don't know if it has anything to do with nature or nurture, but there are different expectations in terms of how a female leader versus a male leader ought to behave.

> THE IDEA: A certain amount of self-promotion is
> required to gain leadership visibility and in certain
> demographics, in order to attain best mix of diversity
> in the team, you may have to sponsor a selected
> group of leaders, e.g. women and ethnic minorities
> and actively seek growth opportunities for them.

What advice would you give to female leaders who are going to be managing partners?

Stay authentic – find out your signature leadership style and stay true to yourself. Only when you are being yourself can you be the best you can be. When you try to pretend to be somebody else, it never works. Your effectiveness drops because people see through you and know it is not genuine. When I try to copy someone, I feel it does not work for me and that's when I start feeling more insecure. I have to remind myself that it's not about looking like someone but about what I represent, how I can become the best me and accomplish what I need to in my profession or in any role.

LEADING THE ORGANISATION

Where Korn Ferry is concerned, what are the top challenges it is going through at the moment?

Korn Ferry is going through a major transformation – we are now the world's largest executive search firm, the world's largest leadership and talent consulting firm. This began about 12 years ago when Korn Ferry decided to become a public listed company. We can't just remain as an executive search firm because there is a natural limitation to how big we can be. We created a new strategy and vision for Korn Ferry – we wanted to be an end-to-end talent consulting firm, of which executive search and recruitment plays a big part, in addition to talent and leadership development. With that, we've acquired a number of global brands to consolidate the industry and develop the world's largest consulting firm.

The next phase of the journey that we are currently embarking on is the integration of our three divisions – executive search, leadership and talent consulting, and recruitment process outsourcing. When we go to any client, we want to be able to use all our tools to assess leadership talent, to help with the pipeline and leadership development programmes and to help design and implement leadership development programmes. We want our clients to see us as an integrated one-stop service firm, and that they have access to our many different aspects and capabilities. This requires a different mindset from that of change management. It also requires a different skill set – we need partners who are very familiar with all three sides of our business. With that, we have brought in a lot of new leaders and younger talent that have those capabilities.

THE IDEA: In this age of constant search for efficiency and effectiveness, explore areas in your businesses where you can integrate capabilities and provide an one-stop solution for your clients.

How do you create this new reality and how do you transition the organisation?

We have to create new propositions and constantly reinvent ourselves. We have been evolving. It's not so much about who you know anymore, but your ability to assess whether an executive fits the challenge of the organisation that you are recruiting for. We used a lot of intellectual properties (IPs) that we have acquired to assess external talent. We also assess internal talent and sometimes compare them to pick the best leader for the organisation – you cannot do this on LinkedIn. The solution-oriented and unbiased points of view as well as the IPs help us to gauge a candidate's motivation and leadership style against the fit of the organisation.

We are in the process of consolidating and taking the best of every approach, getting rid of some overlaps and creating a cohesive and comprehensive set of tools for performance management, individual assessment and leadership development. We are creating new services, new programmes and new ways of applying some of these tools to help solve client issues around talent and leadership. We have to innovate, think of new ways of doing things and be trained using new tools.

How is it different being in an Asian sector of a global MNC? What are some attributes that an Asian leader needs to successfully manage this sector?

More than ever, being Asian or being in Asia is really good for an MNC. Asian businesses used to represented less than 10% of the global revenues of a lot of US or European MNCs. This is changing very fast and no global company can ignore Asia as a business opportunity. The challenge comes when you have to be local and global at the same time. A lot of MNCs struggle with connectivity to headquarters or other countries – when you are too local, there is too much of a gap in terms of culture and communication between the local talent and the regional or global talent. It is about creating an international mindset.

There is definitely a growing number of Asians who are now operating at an international level. In the past, Western expatriates in Asia were the only internationalists, now there's a huge number of Asians who are internationalists who have worked in many different countries in Asia and studied in Western countries. This combination is incredibly powerful. It is no longer about whether you are Asian or not, the question is whether you are international enough.

> THE IDEA: **Combine your innate Asian experience and know-how with the best attributes of internationalisation in terms of social and communication skills to gain a powerful advantage.**

What are some key attributes that would help a person to secure an Asian leadership role?

When you are at the beginning of your career, the things that would make you successful are your task-orientation and your ability to get things done. You need to be very adept in following directions and complying. Your social skills are less important. As you get to director level and beyond, your ability to complete tasks and follow directions are less required, while your ability to socialise and be participative and creative become very important. All the hard skills that you acquired in the earlier part of your career and got you to middle management are now less vital and you will need to acquire a whole new set of skills to operate more strategically.

> THE IDEA: **The skills that made you successful as a middle manager may end up as stumbling blocks as you proceed higher up the leadership food chain. Always have a realistic assessment of your competency gaps every two to three years and look for ways to skill up for the next job.**

In terms of the candidates that you've met, what tends to be lacking that hinders them from taking up a more senior leadership position?

Leaders have to be talent magnets. When you hire a good leader into an organisation, there's often a big following of people into the organisation. Being a talent magnet also means that you need to have good talent lenses as a leader and put a lot of focus on developing and grooming new leaders. You need to grow the smartest and best team.

A lot of Asian leaders don't quite make that connection. There's so much focus on academic education and being smart that I think a lot of social skills get stunted. You have to realise that it's your ability to inspire someone to work really hard for you, and that is what is going to make you a great leader. It's not just working hard yourself. You have to have the multiplier effect – good leaders produce other good leaders. This defines your potential in terms of how big you are going to be as a leader. A leader's job is to create talent and not just be the talent.

> THE IDEA: At different stages of your leadership journey, the focus on various competencies for success will evolve. Ultimately, the organisational leader needs to move beyond being a talent to being a talent magnet to attract others who may be far more capable than them.

Do you have insights about the difference between promoting someone from within and jettisoning someone from outside? What are some of the pros and cons of doing either or both?

Many studies have shown that there is a very high risk of failure when you jettison someone very senior from the outside. There is higher success rate and longer tenure rate when you appoint CEOs from within rather than externally. Companies only look externally when they do not have the bench, it's something they do when necessary. That said, there have been some fantastic turnarounds from companies that have been renewed by leaders from outside who bring new ideas, new visions and new ways of doing things.

You can't say that one is better than the other, you have to look at the holistic picture and figure out what is best for the organisation and the future of the company. You also need to figure out the kind of leader you need and if there is a leader from within the organisation. If you have the right leaders within the organisation, you are much better off appointing one from within. If you need desperate change of direction and culture, bringing in an external leader is sometimes the best thing you need even though you might have the right leader internally. If the company is not going in the right direction, a great internal leader's ability to change direction and gear could be limited. You have to assess critically and independently what is needed for an organisation and consider all options to come up with an optimal solution.

THE IDEA: Promote from within if you can, unless you need a fresh new perspective in reorganising and reenergising the business and team.

What are some of the best practices in working with organisations?

The companies that are really focused on talent development are very strategic about drawing out people with high potential and then matching them to suitable roles. Great companies can identify the potential CEO early on in their careers. They are then very strategic about putting these individuals into certain assignments and projects that will expand and test their capabilities. It is one thing to identify and assess them, but it is another thing to put them to the test and see how they fare. It involves having an entire talent strategy and plan and the investment appetite to make it happen instead of being of reactive. A lot of companies are reactive because they are busy.

Great organisations that are talent machines live and breathe talent management. They measure how effective you are as a leader in terms of grooming your own teams. Talent management ensures that your company has the choice of best leaders. The rest of the business happens because they have the right talent. Very successful large companies that operate globally invest a lot on talent – it's not just a lip-service nor is it accidental – they really go out of their way to groom and develop their talent and produce their leaders.

> THE IDEA: The war for talent never ceases.
> Organisations that are moving from "good" to
> "great" need to put in place a robust talent strategy
> and talent management system and dare to invest
> in their people. It is better to invest in talent (even
> though they may still leave) than to not invest in
> talent who still end up staying in your organisation!

CONCLUSION:
LEADERSHIP IN PERSPECTIVE

In my first book entitled *Career Conversations*, I wanted to find answers and advice about what makes a successful career professional and after interviewing 20 professionals from all walks of life, I realised that the keys to success lie in the 5Cs: Clarity, Commitment, Courage, Communication and Connections. Answering the question of what makes a great leader was made infinitely more difficult by the fact that there is no one-size-fits all definition to leadership. Having heard the perspectives of these 16 leaders whom I interviewed, the following are some of the gathered insights that clarify the myriad definitions of this term:

- Leadership is the ability to inspire motivation in others to move toward a desirable vision, to the extent that it becomes a shared effort, a shared vision and a shared success.

- Leadership requires harnessing the energy and efforts of a group of individuals to move them from an unremarkable Point A to a very desirable Point B. And in that process, the group of individuals becomes a team.

- Leadership is not about having a type of personality trait but a decision to take a stand or step in order to encourage, inspire or motivate others to move with you.

- Effective leaders do not rely on their title or positional power to lead. Instead, they use their own personal power combined with strategic influence to win the hearts and minds of followers.

- Leadership is influencing others with your character, humility and by example. It is an belief that through serving others, others would willingly be led by you.

- Leadership is the ability to take an average team of individuals and transform them into superstars.
- Management is focused on tasks, leadership is focused on the person.

One of my favorite leadership quotes comes from an Afghan proverb that says, "If you think you're leading and no one is following you, then you're only taking a walk." While it sounds almost common sense that leaders need followers in order to get things done, there are often accounts of leaders abusing their authority and positional titles to ensure followership. In Asia, we acknowledge that while hierarchies are prevalent and adhered to for followership, it is relationships that play an especially important role in how to go about our business dealings and how we lead our teams. The main differentiator that distinguishes top leaders from others is not their intellectual ability but their intrapersonal and interpersonal abilities to be self-aware and influence others towards a shared vision.

Every one of the leaders I have interviewed has dedicated their lives to building their careers, people whom they work with and their organisations towards excellence. They are noted leaders in their respective fields that include politics and social enterprise to banking and manufacturing. From these conversations, I have distilled six attributes/competencies that leaders in Asia can do more of, as well as a LEADER process to deal with leadership challenges.

L – Listen & Learn

While some may be impressed with how well you speak, the right people will be impressed with how well you listen. Great leaders are great listeners – they listen proactively with strategic intention and look out for what is "not said". In this current era where information is readily available at the touch of a keypad, these leaders understand that beyond information, crucial knowledge and wisdom are gained by listening and engaging with others, not machines. Listening is a prerequisite for learning and continuous learning is essential for a leader to motivate and influence others.

Phyllis Cheung, the Managing Director for McDonald's China, summarised the importance of this concept well when she related her experience of leaders who may not be seen as strategic thinkers doing very well because they are able to extract values and strategic ideas by actively listening to people. Jonathan Asherson, Regional Director for Rolls-Royce, places such importance on the art of listening when he advocates that leaders must listen to the last "drop" and really get it, and repeat it with clarity. In a university setting where you are surrounded by academics who all have PhDs, Arnoud De Meyer, President at Singapore Management University, understands this acutely and talks about the need for "collaborative leadership". However, he also warns about the dangers of over-listening to others which may lead to procrastination and being too flexible and may result in a lack of clarity of purpose in terms of aims and vision.

Being a leader should not be viewed as a licence to dominate the stage and speak at will but instead as giving space and permission to others to voice their opinions. In this age of instant communication, everyone seems to be in such a rush to communicate what's on their mind that they fail to realise the value of everything that can be gleaned from the minds of others. Most leaders fail to understand that the purpose of communication is not to message but to engage, which requires listening. Don't be fooled into thinking that being heard is more important than hearing. The first rule in communication is to seek understanding before seeking to be understood. The leaders I interviewed constantly shared with me the insights gleaned when they listened intently, not just to their closer executive members, but to the lower levels of the organisation, where they really knew what was working (or not) with the company.

Here are some tips to becoming a better leader listener:

1. **Make listening your core competency.** One of the best compliments you can receive as a leader is to be known as a good listener. Being recognised in this skill will open doors, surface opportunities, bridge differences and take you places that talking never could. Listening demonstrates that you respect others, and is the first step in building trust and rapport.

2. **Listen to non-verbals.** People say as much (if not more) with their actions, inactions, body language, facial expressions, etc., as they do with their verbal communication. Don't be lulled into thinking that just because someone is not saying something, they're not communicating. In fact, most people won't overtly verbalise opposition or disagreement, but they will almost always deliver a very clear message with their non-verbal communication.

3. **Pay attention to what is not being said.** This is the auditory equivalent of "reading between the lines." If a member of your staff gushes approval for your project's objectives, but doesn't comment on the plan to accomplish those objectives, he or she may have issues with the process. Or, he or she may be in agreement with the process and therefore feels no need to comment. It's up to you to ask questions and get clarity on what is not being said.

4. **You should never be too busy to listen.** Set aside one hour of your busy schedule once a day to meet with someone new within the organisation. Disregard the position and seniority of the audience as wisdom does not just come from peers and those above you – it can come from anywhere at anytime, but only if you're willing to listen. Expand your sphere of influence and learn from those with different perspectives and experiences.

5. **Listen for opportunity.** Intuitive listeners look for the story behind the message, and the opportunity beyond the issue. Listening is about discovery, and discovery doesn't just impact the present – it can also influence the future.

6. **Recognise the contributions of others.** One of the most often overlooked aspects of listening is thanking others for their contributions. If you derive benefits from listening to someone, thank them with a commitment to act on their ideas. Even if no value is perceived, thank them for their time and input. Never forget to acknowledge those who contribute energy, ideas, actions or results. Few things go as far in building goodwill as recognising others.

7. **Actively seek out dissenting opinions and thoughts.** Listen to those that confront you, challenge you, stretch you and develop you. True wisdom doesn't see opposition, only opportunity. I believe it was Benjamin Franklin who said, "Speak little, do much."

E – Empathise

In the *Harvard Business Review* article "What Leaders Really Do", John Kotter writes, "Motivation and inspiration energize people, not by pushing them in the right direction as control mechanisms do but by satisfying basic human needs for achievement, a sense of belonging, recognition, self-esteem, a feeling of control over one's life, and the ability to live up to one's ideals. Such feelings touch us deeply and elicit a powerful response." In these current times where engaged workers are the exception rather than the norm, there is a cry for emphatic leaders to lead the rising generation of Gen Y workers.

Koh Poh Tiong, Chairman of Ezra Holdings, exemplifies these values deeply when he responded to the question of why he dedicates so much time to charitable causes, "The sick cannot help the sick; and the poor cannot help the poor. We, who are blessed with much, have a duty to take care of those who are suffering around us. It is more blessed to give than to receive." I personally felt the impact of his kindness when he insisted on walking me out of the office, through the corridor and to the lift lobby – an act he performs regardless of who visits him each day. William Wan, General Secretary at Singapore Kindness Movement, advocates that a good leader should love the people he leads, believe in the people he leads and enjoy being with them. Leaders lead because they care and not just to promote themselves.

A formal definition of empathy is the ability to identify and understand another's situation, feelings and motives. It is our capacity to recognise the concerns other people have. Empathy means "putting yourself in the other person's shoes" or "seeing things through someone else's eyes". Years ago, I came across a saying that went something like this: "The measure of a man (or woman) is how they treat someone who is of absolutely no use to them. Empathy should not be selective: It should be a daily habit."

Although the concept of empathy might contradict the modern concept of a traditional workplace – competitive, cut-throat and with employees climbing over each other to reach the top – the reality is that for business leaders to be successful, they need to not just see or hear the activity around them, but also relate to the people they serve. I felt this level of empathy the strongest during my conversations with Mr Koh Poh Tiong and Mr William Wan. Apart from was said during the meeting, both of them insisted on walking me out to the lift lobby and waited till I went in before leaving. To me, that was empathy in action with plenty of humility.

While empathy is a right-brain activity, it is far from being a touchy-feely topic. At its core, empathy is the lubricant that keeps relationships running smoothly. Empathy is a valued currency that allows us to create bonds of trust and gives us insights into what others may be feeling or thinking; it sharpens our "people acumen" and informs our decisions.

There are numerous studies that link empathy to business results. They include studies that correlate empathy with increased sales, with the performance of the best managers of product development teams and with enhanced performance in an increasingly diverse workforce. Along those lines, in Daniel Pink's book, *A Whole New Mind: Moving from the Information Age to the Conceptual Age*, he predicts that power will reside with those who have strong right-brain (interpersonal) qualities. He cites three forces that are causing this change: Abundance, Asia and Automation. "Abundance" refers to our increasing demand for products or services that are aesthetically pleasing, "Asia" refers to the growing trend of outsourcing to the region and "Automation" is self-explanatory. In order to compete in the new economy market, Pink suggests six areas that are vital to our success. One of these is empathy; the ability to imagine yourself in someone else's position, to imagine what they are feeling, to understand what makes people tick, to create relationships and to be caring of others – all of which are very difficult to outsource or automate, and yet is increasingly important to business.

Empathy is also particularly critical to leadership development in this age of young, independent, highly marketable and mobile workers. In a popular *Harvard Business Review* article entitled "What Makes a Leader?", Dr Daniel Goleman isolates three reasons why empathy is so important: the increasing use of teams (which he refers to as "cauldrons of bubbling emotions"), the rapid pace of globalisation (with cross cultural communication easily leading to misunderstandings) and the growing need to retain talent, especially when managing the Gen Y workers. "Leaders with empathy," states Goleman, "do more than sympathize with people around them: they use their knowledge to improve their companies in subtle, but important ways." This doesn't mean that they agree with everyone's view or try to please everybody. Rather, they "thoughtfully consider employees' feelings – along with other factors – in the process of making intelligent decisions."

So this leads me to a question that I am sometimes asked: "Can you teach someone to be empathetic?" We all know people who are naturally and consistently empathetic – these are the people who can easily forge positive connections with others. They are people who use empathy to engender trust and build bonds; they are catalysts who are able to create positive communities for the greater good. But even if empathy does not come naturally to some of us, I firmly believe that we can develop this capacity.

Here are a few practical tips leaders can apply that build on what was mentioned in the book regarding the importance of listening:

1. **Listen to build trust.** People do not care how much you know, unless they know how much you care through the way you listen and respond. Active listening is paying close attention to *who* is saying *what* and *how* they're saying it. It involves listening to the content of the message and discerning how the speaker is feeling about the topic he or she is discussing. The content is often straightforward and easy enough to grasp, but determining the speaker's emotional stance usually takes practice.

2. **Never justify or interrupt others when listening.** Nothing stops others from sharing the truth with you than when you refute their opinions or say something like "I know" or "but you are wrong". Don't listen to have your opinions validated or your ego stroked, listen to be challenged and to learn something new. You're not always right, so stop pretending you know everything and humble yourself to others. If you desire to be listened to, then give others the courtesy of listening to them.

3. **Adding value to what you have heard.** Validate the speaker's feelings and opinions without agreeing or disagreeing to show that you are listening and empathise: "I understand how you could feel like that." Summarise what you have heard the speaker say, focusing on the facts, to convey that you comprehend: "If I understand you correctly, you are saying that..."

4. **Encourage genuine perspective-taking.** Managers consistently should put themselves in the other person's shoes. As Atticus Finch in Harper Lee's *To Kill a Mockingbird* famously said: "You can never understand someone unless you understand their point-of-view, climb in that person's skin or stand and walk in that person's shoes." For managers, this includes taking into account the personal experience or perspective of their employees. It also can be applied to solving problems, managing conflicts or driving innovation.

5. **Remember names.** When interacting with others, always remember their names, or better yet, that of their spouse and children. When your team members see that you care about their close ones, they will automatically draw closer to you.

6. **Be fully present when you are with people.** Don't check your email, look at your watch or take phone calls when a direct report drops into your office to talk to you. Put yourself in their shoes. How would you feel if your boss did that to you? The best leaders physically remove themselves from the computer in order to demonstrate to their staff the importance of the conversation.

7. **Smile at people.** How you show your emotions in the office has a direct impact on the motivation and engagement of your employees, which in turn has a direct impact on their drive and even creativity!

8. **Give genuine recognition and praise.** Pay attention to what people are doing and catch them doing the right things. When you give praise, spend a little effort to make your genuine words memorable: "You are an asset to this team because..."; "This was pure genius"; "I would have missed this if you hadn't picked it up."

9. **Take a personal interest in people.** Show people that you care, and genuine curiosity about their lives. Ask them questions about their hobbies, their challenges, their families, their aspirations. When the situation calls for assistance, ask team members "How can I help with...", "Let me know if you need to..."

Empathy is an emotional and thinking muscle that becomes stronger the more we use it. Try some of these suggestions and watch the reactions of those you work with. I believe you will notice some positive results.

A – Analyse & Anticipate

Leaders are constantly faced with complex and sometimes conflicting information. The need to analyse and synthesise this information in VUCA (Volatile, Uncertain, Complex, Ambiguous) environments becomes exceedingly important in our competitive environments.

Analysis is a process of discovery of the facts, finding out what you know about the situation. One of the most important aspects of analysing any situation is involving the right people. Mr Max Loh, Regional Managing Partner at EY, spoke about this when he mentioned the importance of bringing a diversity of views into his management committee in order to make the best possible decision for the firm. Bernard Tan, President of the Commercial Business Group at ST Kinetics, speaks about the need to sense-make, which is a process to understand your competitors, customers, evolving technology, new regulations and other market dynamics in order to form a view of the changes needed.

Perhaps the best way to harness the power of collective analysis is to start with asking the right questions. When confronted with a new problem or opportunity, a leader can begin by asking:

- **Who knows?** - about the situation/opportunity, or who has the information we need to solve it/realise it.
- **Who cares?** - that something is done about it.
- **Who can?** - do something about the solution.

These questions are fundamental management tips. They help us to identify the people who need to come together, in order to take appropriate action to solve an issue or realise an opportunity. When these fundamental questions are addressed, the leader can now undertake a more detailed approach to examine the situation. The following are some tips for leaders on problem analysis and interpretation of findings:

1. Focus on the root causes of a problem rather than the symptoms. Apply the "five whys" coined by Sakichi Toyoda, the founder of Toyota. (e.g. "Sales turnover has dropped 5% quarter on quarter" – "Why?" – "Because clients are switching to our competitors" – "Why?", and so on.)

2. List assumptions affecting decision-making in your business that are seemingly ingrained (e.g. "We cannot make a better product without increasing R&D costs"). List at least three possible explanations for what you're observing and invite perspectives from diverse stakeholders.

3. Encourage debate by holding "safe zone" meetings where open dialogue and conflict are expected and welcomed.

4. Create a rotating chairperson position at meetings for the clear purpose of questioning the status quo. Appoint naysayers or "Black Hats" at meetings whose roles are to challenge assumptions and ingrained ideas.

5. Force yourself to zoom in on the details and out to see the big picture. At times that may mean physically stepping away from the situation to exercise, look at art, put on non-traditional music, etc. to promote an open mind.

6. Actively look for missing information and evidence that disconfirms your hypothesis.

7. Supplement observation with quantitative analysis.

Leaders who have utilised the above tools of analyses can now leverage on the knowledge gained and start to recognise patterns, push through ambiguity, seek new insights and be a step ahead of competitors to anticipate trends and movements.

Tips to improve your ability to anticipate:

1. Talk to clients, suppliers and other partners to understand their situation and challenges.

2. Conduct market research and business simulations to understand competitors' perspectives, gauge their likely reactions to new initiatives and products.

3. Use scenario planning to imagine various futures and prepare for the best and worst case scenarios.

4. Look at your closest competitors and evaluate what actions they could take to upset your strategies.

5. List clients you have lost and gained recently to try to figure out what you can do more or less of to gain market share.

6. Attend conferences and networking events both within and outside your field of expertise.

D – Decide

The next phase in our LEADER approach after the analysis phase is to consider the number of solutions and to make the best informed decisions. In uncertain times, decision makers may have to make tough calls with incomplete information, and they must often do so quickly. The best strategic thinkers insist on multiple options from the outset and don't get prematurely locked into simplistic go/no-go choices. They don't shoot from the hip but follow a disciplined process that balances rigour with speed, considers the trade-offs involved and takes both short- and long-term goals into account. In the end, strategic leaders must have the courage of their convictions, informed by a robust decision process.

Sylvia Lim, Chairperson for the Workers' Party, speaks about four frames to consider when making decisions about organisational change. The first is the *structural* frame, which involves the architecture of the organisation, how you divide roles, how you integrate the different roles, how information flows, etc. The *human resource* frame uncovers how you get the best out of people, whether it is through empowerment, through putting people in the right places, through reward systems or development opportunities. There is also the *political* frame – in an environment where people are competing for resources, how do you navigate these and decide what is the best allocation? The last frame, which I think is the most powerful frame, is the *symbolic* frame. It means that you have to give people something that they can use as a guiding light to move them to another level. This can be overarching principles, credo, stories or a tagline that inspires them to greater heights.

To improve your ability to decide:

1. Reframe binary decisions by explicitly asking your team, "What other options do we have?"
2. Divide big decisions into pieces to understand component parts and better anticipate unintended consequences.
3. Tailor your decision criteria to long-term versus short-term projects.
4. Let others know where you are in your decision process. Are you still seeking divergent ideas and debate, or are you moving toward closure and choice?

5. Determine who needs to be directly involved and who can influence the success of your decision.
6. Consider pilots or experiments instead of big bets, and make staged commitments.

It's also likely that more than one idea may be viable and leaders need clear criteria to select the best idea to implement. Management consultant Peter Drucker has proposed a powerful way to do this in the form of three filter tests to derive a desirable decision:

1. **Operational validity** – Can you take action on this idea, or can you only talk about it? Can you really do something right away to bring about the kind of future you desire?
2. **Economic validity** – Will the idea produce economic results? What would be the early indicators that it was working?
3. **Personal commitment** – Do you really believe in the idea? Do you really want to be that kind of people, do that kind of work and run that kind of business?

E – Execute

Having decided on the best course of action, it is the leader's imperative to act on the decisions and work towards the goal. When interviewed regarding the current business challenges that impede flawless execution, several of the leaders commented on the speed and extent of change they had to grapple with and the need to gear their people to accept and adapt to these changes. Demand for deep, sustainable change in organisations is being driven hard by forces from all directions. Radical disruptions to competition, regulation, technology and client expectations are creating an almost constant need for change. Shareholders are demanding more from fewer resources. Leaders need to empower employees to find new ways to enhance profitability, innovation, business performance and competitive advantage, faster than ever before.

Alicia Yi, Managing Director at Korn Ferry, speaks about the need to create new propositions and constantly reinvent and evolve leaders as well as their businesses before competitors force us to. Jonathan Asherson, Regional Director at Rolls-Royce, reiterates that the challenge of seamless execution lies in managing cost efficiencies while at the same time looking for ways to innovate and improve.

Research consistently reveals high failure rates for transformational change initiatives. According to many independent studies, seven out of ten change efforts that are critical to organisational success fail to achieve their intended results. Independent IT research firm Gartner Group reports that for major corporate systems investments:

- 28% are abandoned before completion.
- 46% are behind schedule or over budget.
- 80% are not used in the way they were intended to be or not used at all six months after installation.

Ultimately, these failures or partial successes were poorly executed due to the lack of change leadership. The world is crying out for leaders who not only "walk the talk" but are able to walk the entire distance without flinching under pressure. People are more likely to understand and energetically support an initiative when they observe leadership behaviour that is both credible and supportive. When change leadership is strong, people can move more quickly from understanding the initiative to supporting it. When change leadership and influence are weak, people may not believe the change is worth supporting or investing energy in. They become more likely to focus efforts on maintaining the status quo rather than moving forward. This is particularly true if there is a legacy of poorly implemented change, which has undermined credibility in the organisation's change leadership.

There are many theories about how to execute change. Many originate with leadership and change management guru, John Kotter. A professor at Harvard Business School and world-renowned change expert, Kotter introduced his eight-step change process in his 1995 book, *Leading Change*. Here's a summary of his eight steps for leading change below:

Step 1: Create Urgency

For change to happen, it helps if the entire company really wants it. Develop a sense of urgency around the need for change. This may help you spark the initial motivation to get things moving.

This isn't simply a matter of showing people poor sales statistics or talking about increased competition. Begin an honest and convincing dialogue about what's happening in the marketplace and with your competition. If many people start talking about the change you propose, the urgency can build and feed on itself.

What change leaders can do:

- Identify potential threats, and develop scenarios showing what could happen in the future.
- Examine opportunities that should, or could, be exploited.
- Start honest discussions, and give dynamic and convincing reasons to get people talking and thinking.
- Request support from customers, outside stakeholders and industry people to strengthen your argument.

Kotter suggests that for change to be successful, 75 per cent of your company's management needs to "buy into" the change. In other words, you have to work really hard on Step 1, and spend significant time and energy on building urgency, before moving on to the next steps. Don't panic and jump in too fast because you don't want to risk further short-term losses – if you act without proper preparation, you could be in for a very arduous journey.

Step 2: Form a Powerful Coalition

Convince people that change is necessary. This often takes strong leadership and visible support from key people within your organisation. Managing change isn't enough – you have to lead it.

You can find effective change leaders throughout your organisation – they don't necessarily follow the traditional company hierarchy. To lead change, you need to bring together a coalition, or team, of influential people whose power comes from a variety of sources, including job title, status, expertise and political importance.

Once formed, your "change coalition" needs to work as a team, continuing to build urgency and momentum around the need for change.

What change leaders can do:

- Identify the true leaders in your organisation, as well as your key stakeholders.
- Ask for an emotional commitment from these key people.
- Work on team building within your change coalition.
- Check your team for weak areas, and ensure that you have a good mix of people from different departments and levels within your company.

Step 3: Create a Vision for Change

When you first start thinking about change, there will probably be many great ideas and solutions floating around. Link these concepts to an overall vision that people can easily grasp and remember.

A clear vision can help everyone to understand why you're asking them to do something. When people see for themselves what you're trying to achieve, the directives they're given tend to make more sense.

What change leaders can do:

- Determine the values that are central to the change.
- Develop a short summary (one or two sentences) that captures what you "see" as the future of your organisation.

- Create a strategy to execute that vision.
- Ensure that your change coalition can describe the vision in five minutes or less.
- Practice your "vision speech" often.

Step 4: Communicate the Vision

What you do with your vision after you create it will determine your success. Your message will probably have strong competition from other day-to-day communications within the company, so you need to communicate it frequently and powerfully, and embed it within everything that you do.

Don't just call special meetings to communicate your vision. Instead, talk about it every chance you get. Use the vision to make decisions and solve problems daily. When you keep it fresh in everyone's minds, they'll remember it and respond to it.

It's also important to "walk the talk." What you do is far more important – and believable – than what you say. Demonstrate the kind of behaviour that you want from others.

What change leaders can do:
- Talk often about your change vision.
- Address peoples' concerns and anxieties, openly and honestly.
- Apply your vision to all aspects of operations – from training to performance reviews. Tie everything back to the vision.
- Lead by example.

Step 5: Remove Obstacles

If you follow these steps and reach this point in the change process, you've been talking about your vision and building buy-in from all levels of the organisation. Hopefully, your staff want to get busy and achieve the benefits that you've been promoting.

But is anyone resisting the change? And are there processes or structures that are getting in its way?

Put in place the structure for change, and continually check for barriers to it. Removing obstacles can empower the people you need to execute your vision, and can help move the change forward.

What change leaders can do:

- Identify, or hire, change leaders whose main roles are to deliver the change.
- Look at your organisational structure, job descriptions, and performance and compensation systems to ensure they're in line with your vision.
- Recognise and reward people for making change happen.
- Identify people who are resisting the change, and help them see what's needed.
- Take action to quickly remove barriers (human or otherwise).

Mike Loh, Managing Partner at EY ASEAN, shares his wisdom of handling detractors to change – ensuring full transparency. Leaders need to constantly engage with our people and be as transparent as possible – where we are going? What are we doing? Why we are doing this? What are the benefits to them? Why are they also going to be successful as we embark on this? If it is seen as a top-down decision, followers would not be motivated or empowered.

Step 6: Create Short-Term Wins

Nothing motivates more than success. Give your company a taste of victory early in the change process. Within a short time frame (this could be a month or a year, depending on the type of change), you'll want to have some "quick wins" that your staff can see. Without this, critics and negative thinkers might hurt your progress.

Create short-term targets and not just one long-term goal. You want each smaller target to be achievable, with little room for failure. Your change team may have to work very hard to come up with these targets, but each "win" that you produce can further motivate the entire staff.

What change leaders can do:

- Look for sure-fire projects that you can implement without help from any strong critics of the change.
- Don't choose early targets that are expensive. You want to be able to justify the investment in each project.
- Thoroughly analyse the potential pros and cons of your targets. If you don't succeed with an early goal, it can hurt your entire change initiative.
- Reward the people who help you meet the targets.

Step 7: Build on the Change

Kotter argues that many change projects fail because victory is declared too early. Real change runs deep. Quick wins are only the beginning of what needs to be done to achieve long-term change.

Launching one new product with a new system is great. But if you can launch 10 products, that means the new system is working. To reach that 10th success, you need to keep looking for improvements.

Each success provides an opportunity to build on what went right and identify what you can improve.

What change leaders can do:

- After every win, analyse what went right, and what needs improving.
- Set goals to continue building on the momentum you've achieved.
- Learn about *kaizen*, the idea of continuous improvement.
- Keep ideas fresh by bringing in new change agents and leaders for your change coalition.

Step 8: Anchor the Changes in Corporate Culture

Finally, to make any change stick, it should become part of the core of your organisation. Your corporate culture often determines what gets done, so the values behind your vision must show in the organisation's day-to-day work.

Make continuous efforts to ensure that the change is seen in every aspect of your organisation. This will help give it a solid place in your organisation's culture.

It's also important that your company's leaders continue to support the change. This includes existing staff and new leaders who are brought in. If you lose the support of these people, you might end up back where you started.

What change leaders can do:

- Talk about progress every chance you get. Tell success stories about the change process, and repeat other stories that you hear.
- Include the change ideals and values when hiring and training new staff.
- Publicly recognise key members of your original change coalition, and make sure the rest of the staff – new and old – remembers their contributions.
- Create plans to replace key leaders of change as they move on. This will help ensure that their legacy is not lost or forgotten.

R – Role Modeling

In the earlier segment on Execute, I mentioned extensively Kotter's eight steps for leading change, but no action is more powerful than followers seeing their leader role-modeling the new reality. Leaders should not just be "talking heads" at townhalls or quoted on websites/newspapers, but authentic role models that teach us lessons that are not spoken but observable by "walking the talk."

Mike Loh, Managing Partner for EY ASEAN, spoke about needing to go into the trenches to make your people also want to go into trenches. That does not equate to doing everything yourself, but you have to demonstrate that to the troops. Rod Leaver, APAC CEO of Lend Lease, demonstrates such sensitivities to the Asian perception that employees should not leave the office before the boss that he makes a point to get out of the office at 6pm the latest in order to role-model the importance of prioritisation to his employees. One of the best examples of role-modeling as a leader comes from Jack Sim, Founder of the World Toilet Organisation, who advocates that if you want to be a leader, first be a servant and be willing to make a fool of yourself to experiment with new ideas, and even allow others to claim the credit for your work. Fundamentally, as summarised eloquently by Tan Chuan Jin, Manpower Minister of Singapore, effective role-modeling starts with the self. A leader must be aware of his or her personal values and beliefs, know how to apply and communicate these values or beliefs in his or her area of leadership, and thereby instill 'trust' in their followers, even in times where they may disagree with you.

As part of the "Leading Yourself" section of the interviews, I asked the 16 leaders who their leadership role models were and the lessons they learnt from them. Consistent with what Jim Kouzes and Barry Posner (authors of The Leadership Challenge) collected from their research on leadership role models, most leaders reported that a family member had the most influence on them, followed by business leaders, and finally, teachers or coaches. Kouzes and Posner's research would concur: "The life you lead is the legacy you leave."

As we close our discovery of the LEADER model of inspiring and leading others, I think it is fitting to conclude that there is really no one-size-fit-all version of a leader. The 16 leaders I interviewed come from diverse backgrounds and have their own unique brand of leadership. What is consistent is the level of self-awareness and clarity of purpose they have towards their organisation and the people they lead – in short, their authenticity. Authentic leadership is about being the person you know in your heart you have always been destined to be. Authentic leadership does not come from your title or from the size of your paycheck. Instead, this form of leadership comes from the person that you are.

Here are 10 things that authentic leaders do on a regular basis:

1. **They speak their truth.** In business today, we frequently "swallow our truth". We say things to please others and to look good in front of others. Authentic leaders are different. They consistently speak the truth. They would never betray themselves by using words that are not aligned with who they are. This does not give anyone a licence to say hurtful things. Speaking the truth is simply about being clear, honest and authentic.

2. **They lead from the heart.** Business is about people. Leadership is about people. The best leaders wear their hearts on their sleeves and are not afraid to show their vulnerability. They genuinely care about other people and spend their days developing the people around them. They are like the sun: the sun gives all it has to the plants and the trees. But in return, the plants and the trees always grow toward the sun.

3. **They have rich moral fibre.** Who you are speaks far more loudly than anything you could ever say. Strength of character is true power, and people can feel it a mile away. Authentic leaders work on their character. They walk their talk and are aligned with their core values. They are noble and good. And in doing so, people trust, respect and listen to them.

4. **They are courageous.** It takes a lot of courage to go against the crowd. It takes a lot of courage to be a visionary. It takes a lot of inner strength to do what you think is right

even though it may not be easy. We live in a world where so many people walk the path of least resistance. Authentic leadership is all about taking the road less travelled and doing not what is easy, but what is right.

5. **They build teams and create communities.** One of the primary things that people look for in their work experience is a sense of community. In the old days, our community was where we lived. We would have block parties and street picnics. In the new age of work, employees seek their sense of community and connection from the workplace. Authentic leaders create workplaces that foster human linkages and lasting friendships.

6. **They deepen themselves.** The job of the leader is to go deep. Authentic leaders know themselves intimately. They nurture a strong self-relationship. They know their weaknesses and play to their strengths. And they always spend a lot of time transcending their fears.

7. **They are dreamers.** Einstein said that, "Imagination is more important than knowledge." It is from our imaginations that great things are born. Authentic leaders dare to dream impossible dreams. They see what everyone else sees and then dream up new possibilities. They spend a lot of time with their eyes closed creating blueprints and fantasies that lead to better products, better services, better workplaces and deeper value. How often do you close your eyes and dream?

8. **They care for themselves.** Taking care of your physical dimension is a sign of self-respect. You can't do great things at work if you don't feel great. Authentic leaders eat well, exercise and care for the temples that are their bodies. They spend time with nature, drink plenty of water and get regular massages so that, physically, they are operating at optimum levels of performance.

9. **They commit to excellence rather than perfection.** No human being is perfect. Every single one of us is a work in progress. Authentic leaders commit themselves to excellence in everything that they do. They are constantly pushing the envelope and raising their standards. They do not seek perfection and have the wisdom to know the difference. What would your life look like if you raised your standards well beyond what anyone could ever imagine of you?

10. **They leave a legacy.** To live in the hearts of the people around you is to never die. Success is wonderful but significance is even better. You were made to contribute and to leave a mark on the people around you. In failing to live from this frame of reference, you betray yourself. Authentic leaders are constantly building their legacies by adding deep value to everyone that they deal with and leaving the world a better place in the process.

Does this sound time-consuming for a leader? It is. But as a leader, you should realise that your greatest contribution is the behaviour you cause or allow to thrive in the organisation's upper ranks. It's hard work to answer the all-important question: "What do we expect the leader to do here?" But at your level, it is precisely the behaviour everyone needs to see.

ACKNOWLEDGEMENTS

Jessica Tan, Zenith Chua & Loy Zhihao: Thank you for the tremendous dedication and effort in transcribing the interviews.

My esteemed group of interviewees who generously shared their time and leadership perspectives: Jonathan Asherson, Alan Chan, Phyllis Cheung, Carol Fong, Koh Poh Tiong, Kwek Kok Kwong, Matthew Lang, Rod Leaver, Sylvia Lim, Arnoud De Meyer, Max Loh, Jack Sim, Bernard Tan, Tan Chuan Jin, William Wan and Alicia Yi.

The "connectors" who were instrumental in linking me up with above interviewees: Zenith Chua, Simon Craft, Fu Kia Liang, Kor Bing Keong, Vernon Voon and Dharmendra Yadav.

Eugene Chan: Thank you for providing me much needed refuge so I could work on the book; I am always indebted to your kindness.

Low Waifong: You are so much more than a colleague and friend. I greatly appreciate all the help you have rendered to my work and endeavours.

Isaac: Thanks for inspiring me to becoming a better me each day.

My beloved family, friends, mentors, mentees and colleagues who have made my life, career and weekends so much more than just mediocre!

Finally, to God, the architect of my career and author of my life.

ABOUT THE AUTHOR

Ronald Tay is an experienced international organisational development consultant, consummate speaker, author, coach and educator.

He is currently Executive Director at Nomura International (based in Hong Kong) with a leadership role that oversees a gamut of talent initiatives ranging from leadership development, talent management, learning as well as diversity and inclusion in the Asia-ex Japan region. Previously he was Executive Director with the UBS Business University where his nine years with the firm have seen him through significant career transitions spanning local, regional and global responsibilities. His contributions within the leadership and talent development field have helped UBS win the HRM Best Training and Development Award three years in a row from 2012 to 2014 as well as Employer of Choice in 2014.

A well sought-after facilitator and keynote speaker, he most recently was keynote speaker at the 2015 Training & Development Asia Conference on "Developing Training and Development Professionals", 2014 Future Leader's Summit on the topic of "Career Evolution: Differentiation, Leadership and Success" and at Learning World 2013 on "Developing Effective Leaders – re-examining Leadership Programs and Processes". Ronald also lectures on career management and organisational development at the Singapore Management University and the National University of Singapore and continues to actively mentor ex-students from both universities.

In 2014, he published his first book *Career Conversations*, showcasing the career journeys and advice from 20 leading professionals which was a bestseller in local bookstores.

Ronald's other career transitions have included strategic planning for the Singapore government, taking on the role of Senior Consultant at a regional consulting firm, and serving as the ASEAN Head of Learning for the global cosmetics giant L'Oréal.

Ronald completed his Executive MBA at the University of Southern Illinois with distinctions in all his 11 course modules, earning him the Valedictorian award for best results in his cohort. He also holds a Bachelor of Arts (Honours – Upper Division) degree from the National University of Singapore.